Gimena Romero is an artist and illustrator who specializes in textile graphics. She was born in 1985 and currently lives between Mexico City and Madrid.

Her work has been included in various exhibitions around the world, including Mexico, Brazil, Argentina, France, Portugal, Ukraine and Spain. Gimena has 110,500 followers on Instagram, and runs a workshop on Domestika, where she has over 57,000 students.
Gimena loves life, dogs and biscuits.

Web: estudiogimenaromero.com
@gimenaromero
Estudio Gimena Romero

The Embroidery of Mexico

Gimena Romero
Photographs by Pedro Aragón

The Embroidery of Mexico

A vibrant celebration of traditional and modern designs

SEARCH PRESS

Contents

- 06   Foreword by Georgina Sánchez Celaya
- 08   Introduction: 'If I die far away from you'
- 10   Materials and tools
- 16   Transferring onto the fabric
- 20   Tenango embroidery
- 42   Street embroidery
- 72   Mazahua embroidery
- 112   Toninero embroidery
- 122   Mixe embroidery
- 130   Purépecha embroidery
- 150   Lavín embroidery
- 160   Compositions from texture
- 182   Templates
- 190   Biography, thanks, and list of embroiderers
- 192   Publication details

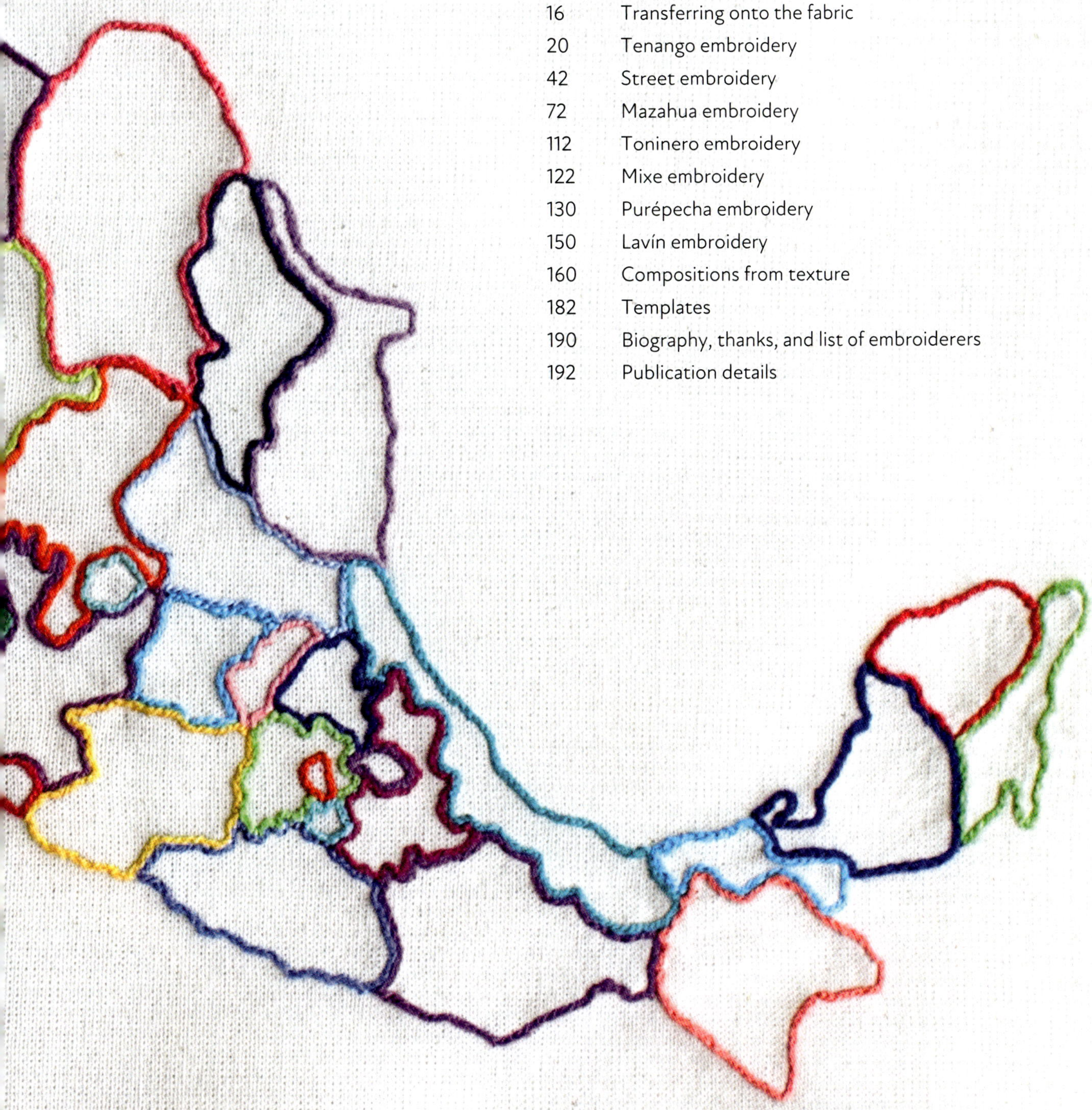

Foreword

By giving a name to a place, an action or indeed an object, we manage to appropriate it for ourselves in a symbolic manner. Through words, Gimena Romero has captured another side of embroidery and shows it in this book in a natural and simple way for those who want to explore the language of embroidery or simply delight in the forms and textures that this art generates.

The Embroidery of Mexico is an invitation to the reader to learn the multiple techniques of embroidery that exist in a country as diverse as Mexico, and in tandem, to start becoming familiar with textile expressions, the world view and the characteristics of the cultures bequeathed to us by this invaluable inheritance. So that this heritage is not lost and remains alive it is necessary for more embroidering hands to appropriate it and reinterpret it in accordance with its social and cultural context, as Gimena Romero has done. Part of this appropriation and reinterpretation is present in the chapter dedicated to street embroidery, a celebration of collective embroidery as a ritual and a form of social coexistence. If this chaotic and gigantic metropolis, Mexico City, is crying out for a form of traditional embroidery, this would be street embroidery, which is done in the community, in the heart of the district, manufactured by *doñitas*[1], the young women who live in neighbourhoods that are devoted to caring for family.

In the chapter dedicated to Lavín embroidery[2], in which the raw material is hair and not thread, the vocation of this book is resumed: to show how the tradition lives on from hand to hand and from mouth to mouth. However, very little of this tradition has been committed to paper, for which reason Gimena Romero has given herself the task of visiting several corners of Mexico to begin an investigation that reveals the secrets of local embroidery and its history.

The book that you have in your hand contains a testimony of various trips that the author has made in order to continue learning to 'speak textile'. This whole learning and knowledge odyssey has been accompanied by Pedro Aragón, friend and accomplice, who has breathed life into this project with beautiful photographs.

[1] Diminutive and affectionate form of *doña* (lady), a word from Spanish-language slang to refer to a married lady.
[2] Lavín embroidery is a very old technique, found in Imperial China, which arrived in Mexico via Spain.

The Argonauts have explored Tzinzuntzan – the former capital of imperial Purépecha – passing through Oaxaca and the Mixe embroidery of the self-named *Ayuujk*. The tour ends in the city of Valle de Bravo, the cradle of adventures and sleepless nights where the author of this book came up against the language of needle and thread of the Deer People: Mazahua embroidery, typical of Mexico state[3]. Without a doubt, I can say that this is one of the most complex and elaborate forms of embroidery that exists in Mexico and one of the most beautiful and difficult in terms of making and craftsmanship.

The Embroidery of Mexico is a document that shows artistic creation not just as an expression of the purest emotion that enchants mankind but also as a method of investigation through which it seeks to preserve the techniques, to give a name to those stitches that have existed in silence for years and in so doing to preserve the richness of the living language which is embroidery. For all of those readers who want to 'speak textile', here is a work produced with much love, developed in the heart of a country overflowing with history, richness and working people who say '*mande*' (a Mexican word used to express a willingness to serve, help or understand) as proof of the nobility that lies in their hearts and not as a sign of submission, a beautiful and beloved country in which we Mexicans want to live in peace and without violence. And if for some strange reason death takes us far away from this land, a thousand and one times may they bring us back here[4].

Georgina Sánchez Celaya
*Researcher, Department of Modern
and Contemporary Art History,
University of Bern (Switzerland).*

---

[3] In Mexico, there are three states with Mazahua settlements: Chihuahua, Michoacán and Mexico state, the last two being the largest and most important. Each state has a distinct type of embroidery, the embroidery that Gimena Romero learned and to which we refer in this book as that of Mexico state.

[4] From a traditional, patriotic mariachi song, *México Lindo y Querido* (*'Beautiful, Beloved Mexico'*), by Chucho Monge, which features the line *'Si muero lejos de ti'* ('If I die far away from you') – see also pages 8–9.

Introduction: 'If I die far away from you'

Speaking about the embroidery of Mexico has strong implications: for history, identity, context, languages and neighbourhoods; it is a Spanish that is not Spanish – it is Mexican, and even poetry.

What is this heritage that is so rich and diverse? In what way does it belong to us? I think of all Mexicans because of what has happened to them: Mexicans who speak in different languages, who eat in different ways, places where the earth is created in different forms and with different names, Mexicans of many skin tones.

I always thought that the inhabitants of Mexico City were cultural orphans. The whole of this investigation through textiles has helped me to discover my identity as Mexican. To find in each new region, in unpronounceable languages, the perennial, the indestructible.

I believe that artistic processes are also a method of investigation and travel, a context and a very useful source for developing a sensitive, visual vocabulary. I understood that firstly I had to assume that I was *mestiza* ('mixed'), and in that way I could learn, fill myself with, and convert myself to, part of a culture as foreign as the words with which all things are named in every place.

I like stories because even though they may be historically false they are authentic in a deeper sense. I spoke to a close friend about how much he likes the Mexican accent and the 'beauty' that he sees in the use of *mande*. Of course, we are not talking about the historic burden contained in this *mande*[1]; we are simply talking about it as a word. It is a pretty way of mediating our history, starting with the spoken word, leaving to one side negative 'historic' words such as despair, disillusionment and death.

---

[1] In Colonial times the word was used subserviently by Mexicans when responding to the foreign colonialists.

I remember that as a child it took a lot of work for me to pronounce the word *patria* ('fatherland'). When I was born, I had no fatherland or grandfathers. I had parents and grandmothers. I was living – sometimes I still live – in a house as large as my childhood world was large. After this time I started to take notice of Avenida de Miguel Ángel de Quevedo (the street I lived on) and the neighbourhood of Chimalistac, where the house still is.

Then Mexico City – which was sometimes a valley and sometimes a lake and is now a monster. And later other cities and other landscapes, even as far as the sea. When I saw the sea they told me that this was where Mexico ended and that beyond this great expanse of water was Europe. It was thus that I learned that 'fatherland' was like the soul of the extension of my room, as if my house extended into towns and mountains, whose names enchanted me with their majestic sound: Cempoaltépetl, Tlahuitoltepec, Huixtán, Chenalhó… and that all of these people who spoke my language and ate the same things as me were also like an extension of my family.

Thus my fatherland, mine, all that was in my hands, in my head and my belly, started to feed off the living and the dead that existed in the province of the personal epic and became ever larger. Heroes that survived with impeccable glory thanks to family memories and experience-based anecdotes. Names like Lázaro Cárdenas, Gilberto Bosques, Ávila Camacho, José Mancisidor, León Felipe, Egon Erwin Kichs, Langston Hughes, Aureliano Álvarez-Coque, José Miaja, Javier Romero, Ana María Rodríguez, Rodrigo Romero and, of course, Carlos Romero, were pronounced as a name, a word, to become a fatherland easier to enunciate. One that is not dignified with the prestige of death but with the celebration of life. But in order to do this we will have to forget the word fear and start to use more needles, more stitches and be a source in all of the languages that we meet on the way. And as the song goes, 'Let them say that I am sleeping and that they [always] bring me here'[2].

[2] *México Lindo y Querido* ('*Beautiful, Beloved Mexico*', a traditional patriotic mariachi song by Chucho Monge).

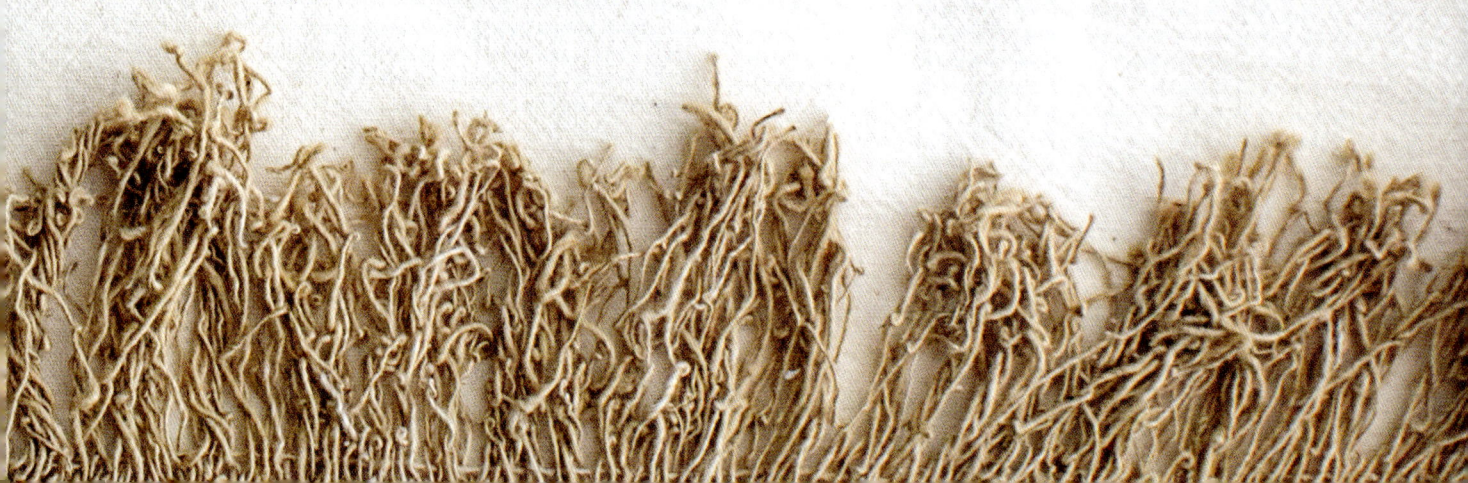

Materials and tools

It is essential to know the names and types of materials necessary for embroidery. There are times when the use of an incorrect needle can break the thread, or a poor-quality hoop may ruin the fabric.
　Embroidery covers every part of the process, not just the fabric. A stitch is formed in every moment through the manipulation of the materials.

Needles

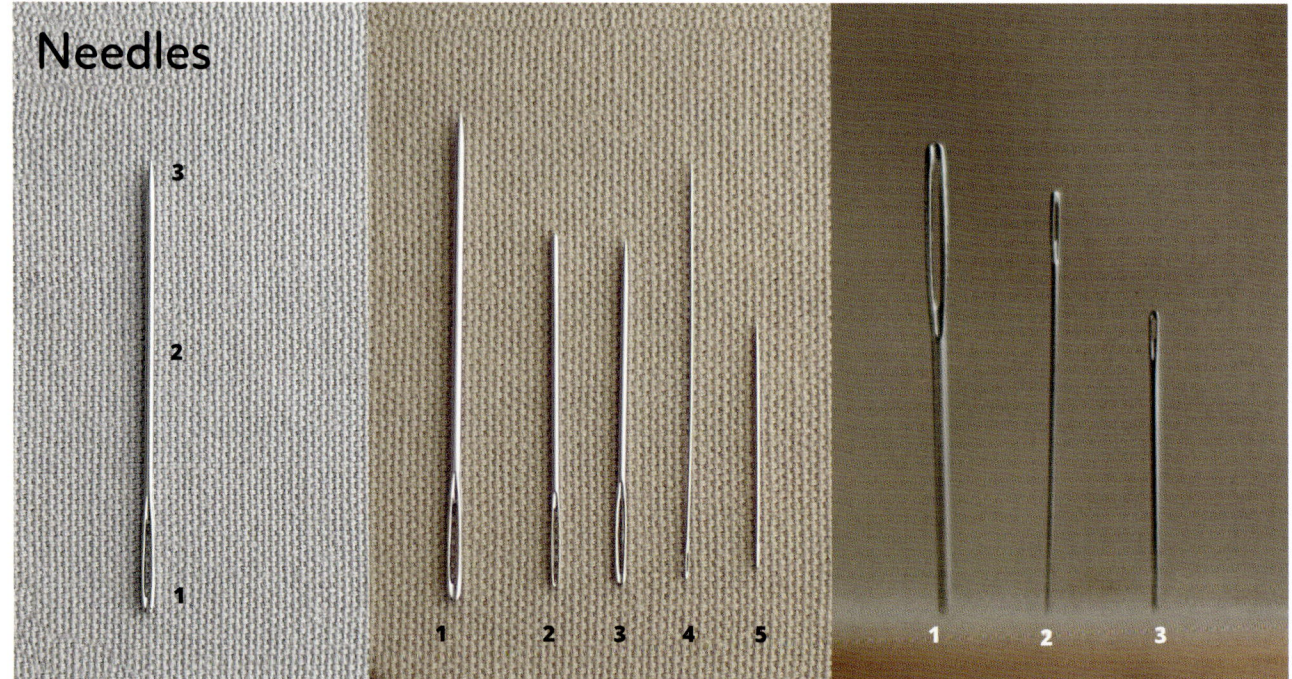

ANATOMY OF A NEEDLE:
1. Eye
2. Shaft/shank (the size or number refers to the body and thickness of the needle)
3. Point

1. Needle with point, large eye, size/no. 22
2. Tapestry/blunt needle
3. Chenille needle (large eye, sharp point)
4. Milliner/straw needle (long and slender)
5. Sharps dressmaking needle

1. Large eye
2. Medium eye
3. Short eye

THE THREADED NEEDLE
The thread that comes from the eye is called the thread tail; the one that comes from the fabric is called the working thread.

I refer to the thickness of the thread as the number of strands. Normally I use a double thread. If this is not the case I refer to the number of single strands.

Example, left: 3 single.

When using double thread, I refer firstly to the number of strands threaded onto the needle and then the total thickness.

Two over four or 2/4
This means that I am using two strands doubled so the final thickness is four strands.

Finally, I refer to the type of thread, which may be sewing, mouliné, perle, mixed, and so on.

For example, 'two over four mouliné', meaning two strands of mouliné embroidery floss on the needle which has been doubled so that the final thickness is four strands.

Threads

1. Mouliné
2. Perlé
3. Sewing
4. Hair
5. Satin

Fabrics

1. Handmade floor-loom canvas
2. Aida/evenweave
3. Linen
4. Canvas
5. Manta (Mexican pure cotton fabric)

Hoops

1. Standing frame
2. Screw frame
3. Spring hoop frame

Scissors

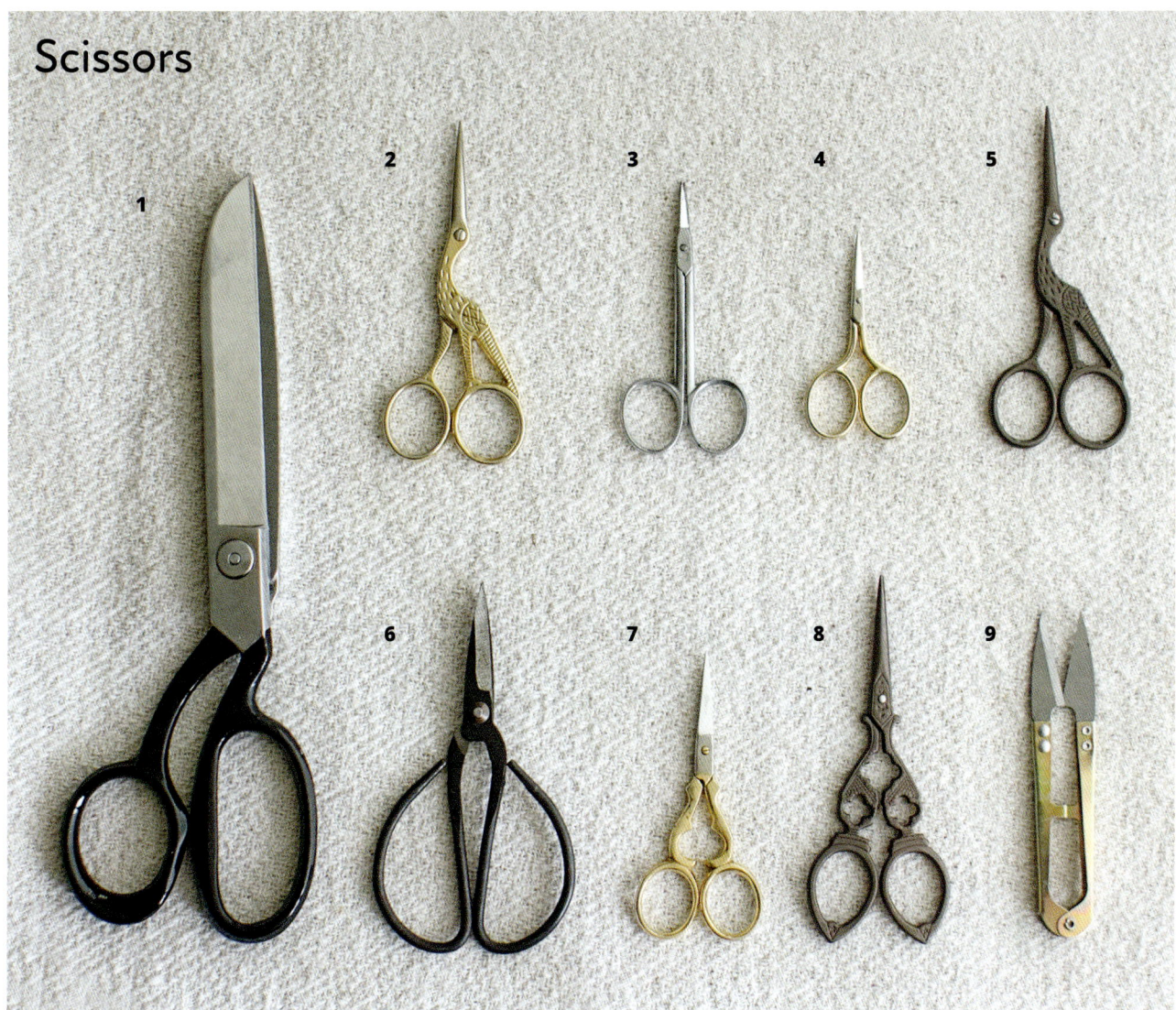

1. Dressmaking shears
2. Classic stork embroidery scissors
3. Nail scissors
4. Short embroidery scissors
5. Black stork embroidery scissors
6. Garden-type scissors
7. Embroidery scissors
8. Ornamental embroidery scissors
9. Thread snips

Dressmaking shears: these new scissors have an excellent edge; they lose it quickly but, if you take care of them, they can last a long time.

Embroidery scissors: embroidery scissors are easily recognizable because they always finish in a sharp point.

Fabric scissors: like dressmaking shears but shorter and without the differentiated thumb and finger holes. Take care of your fabric scissors; I recommend that you invest in a good pair and use them only for cutting fabric.

Nail scissors: these scissors end in a point and have a slightly rounded blade. If you decide to buy some nail scissors for embroidery, use them only for cutting thread and not your nails as well.

Thread snips: an alternative to embroidery scissors, these are very sharp and ideal for cutting close to the work.

Transferring onto the fabric

There are many ways to transfer a motif to fabric in order to embroider. I always transfer using a pencil and medium-weight tracing paper. Alternatively, you can use any transparent or opaque paper. It is simple to do, and requires tools and materials that are easy to obtain in stores and online.

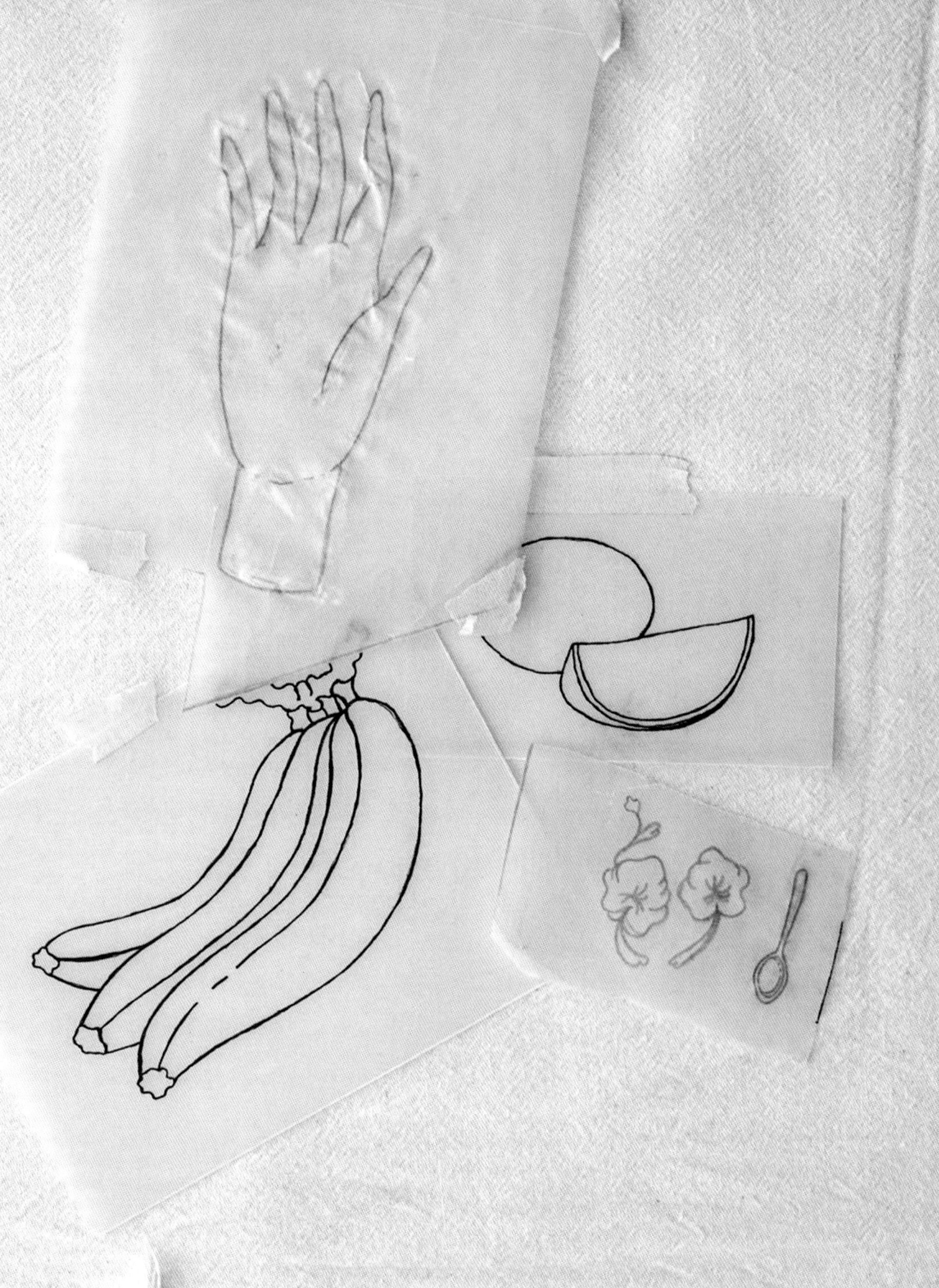

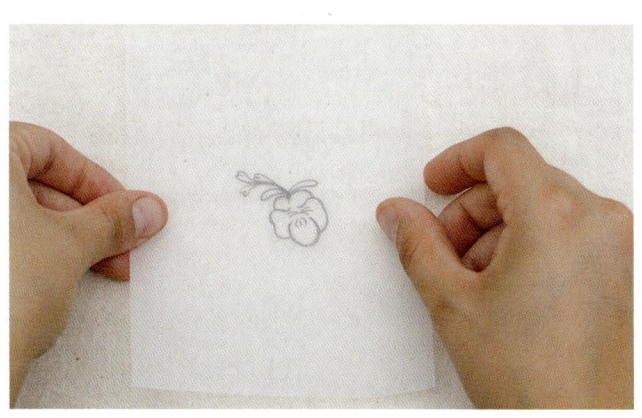

1. On a piece of medium-weight tracing paper (very thick is too opaque and very thin breaks), trace the motif to be transferred. The transfer is done as a mirror image, so remember that the motif will be reversed. If you prefer the way it looks on tracing it (in reverse), simply turn it over and trace over the lines on the other side so that it will be the way you want it when transferred.

2. Make the tracing with a soft pencil – an 8B is ideal.
Lay the paper on the fabric with the graphite side face-down; do this carefully so as not to dirty or stain the fabric.

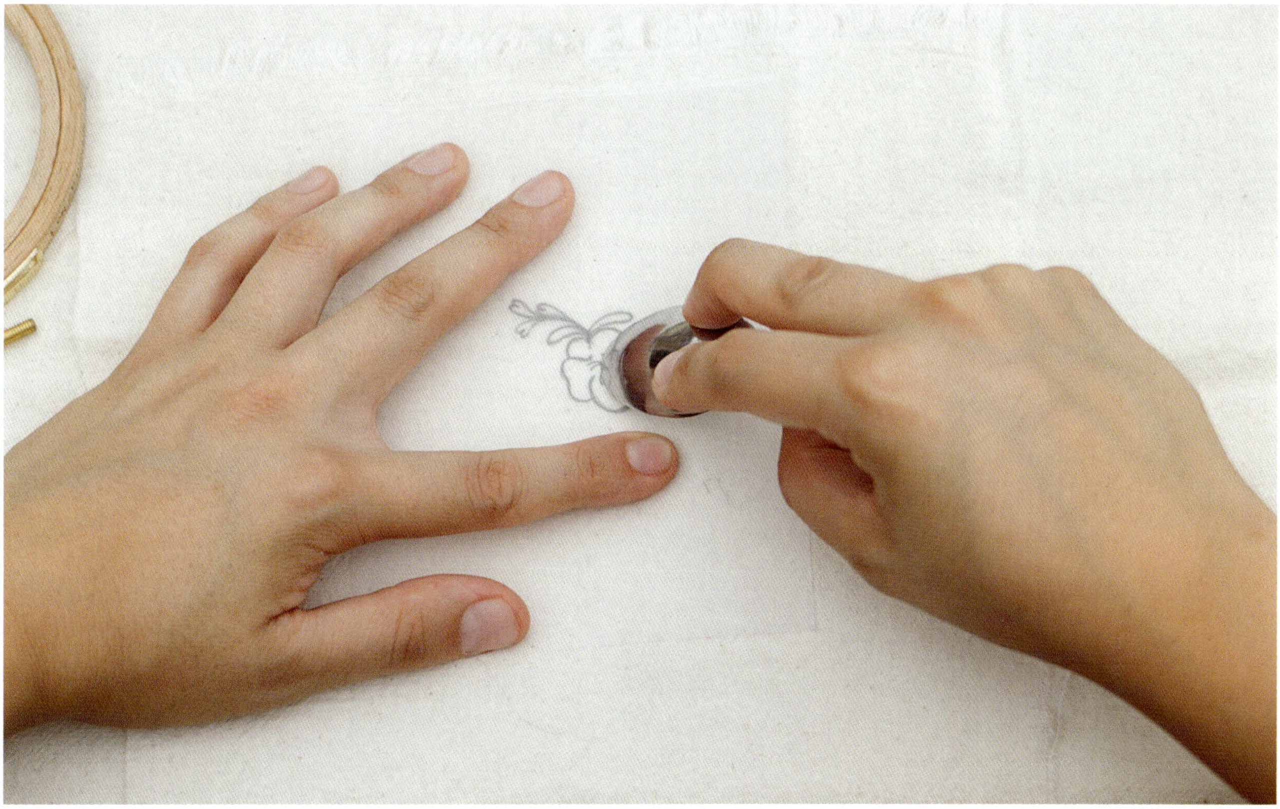

3. Hold the tracing down firmly and with the edge of a spoon rub over the paper, putting pressure on the fabric, to transfer the drawn motif.

4. Spray the fabric with a little fixative to stop the pencil from smudging, and it's ready.

Tenango embroidery

Tenango de Doria, Hidalgo

What can I say about Tenango? Its birds, its flowers, its animals and its land are already part of the landscape of my mind. I could return to Mrs Angélica's house by following the smell of wood from her stove.

When I went to Tenango for the first time, I arrived with a basket of biscuits and a lot of fear. The biscuits were to exchange for stories and the fear had taken me there, but I learned that afterwards. I went to find out about my country's embroidery after being away for a time, although its embroidery had always remained fresh in my memory. I grew up in Coyoacán, a neighbourhood of Mexico City where Tenango embroidery is usually the protagonist in the displays of beautiful handmade things in the artisans' market.

There are sacred places in embroidery and in Tenango there is a veil of silence that taught me to listen in many ways. Here embroidery emerges as a social document and develops into a product for sale as a craft. Whenever I go to investigate a place, I arrive only with the certainty of my ignorance, with humility and total respect. Although Tenango is only 200 kilometres (124 miles) from Mexico City, the distance feels infinite.

Today the stitch most characteristic of Tenango embroidery is the crow's foot. It should be mentioned that in various cultures the name 'crow's foot' is used to describe different stitches. The tradition results from the environment and in Mexico crows and their feet are part of the daily landscape, as in the majority of rural landscapes. To avoid confusion, from here on I refer to this stitch as 'Tenango foot' (see page 22).

After purchasing thread, coming up against ghosts and many other ups and downs, I was left with no biscuits and it was then that I met Mr Manuel and Mrs Angélica, a family that accepted me. I ended up becoming integrated in the community after sharing work and shelter with Mrs Magdalena.

At times I thought that so much mistiness had to do with the use of so many colours, like the grey before dawn. However, nowadays, only Tenango foot is used in all Tenango embroidery, as the *xi* and *hini* stitches are in disuse and have been set aside, because of their great complexity of requiring two needles. It is also because of the lack of interest of new generations in learning the technique. The difference between these stitches and those that require only one needle is minimal, but both are very ornamental stitches.

I have in mind a phrase of Mr Manuel's, the husband of Mrs Angélica (both are embroiderers): 'We, the embroiderers, rise up to move the world. You can keep quiet in order to see if it moves or does not move, or wait for it to move. But we, Miss Gimena, are rising up to move the world'.

These words vibrate in my hands like a cosmic drum, like a clock that does not tell the time. They remind me that, in the end, we never owned time but we lived, sharing it. To embroider together is always to share. Now I am godmother to their children, and I remember that grey, in Tenango, announces the dawn.

After everything, embroidery became a pretext as I was looking for a story. And in the end that story was mine.

STITCHES
Tenango foot

I always describe this stitch as 'walking backwards'. In this type of Otomi[1] embroidery the reverse side is very important. In a good Tenango embroidery the ends are hidden and the result is a continuous line of stitching.

For all the examples that I show in this chapter, I use a three-stranded mouliné cotton thread in a large-eyed no. 22 needle, on a cotton fabric, which is the fabric usually used for this type of work.

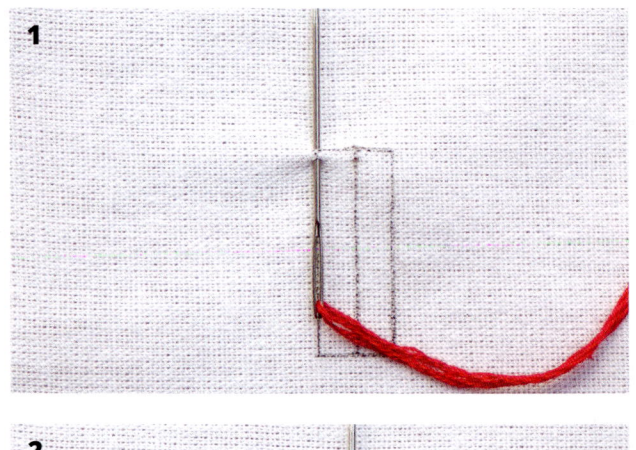

1. When sewing, never make knots and always start on the right side of the fabric. Insert the needle 2–3mm (⅛in) below the top of the shape to be filled. Pull through to leave a short thread end.

2. Reinsert the needle at the other side of the strip being worked to start filling in, and repeat step 1.

[1] Indigenous people who inhabit a fragmented territory in the centre of Mexico.

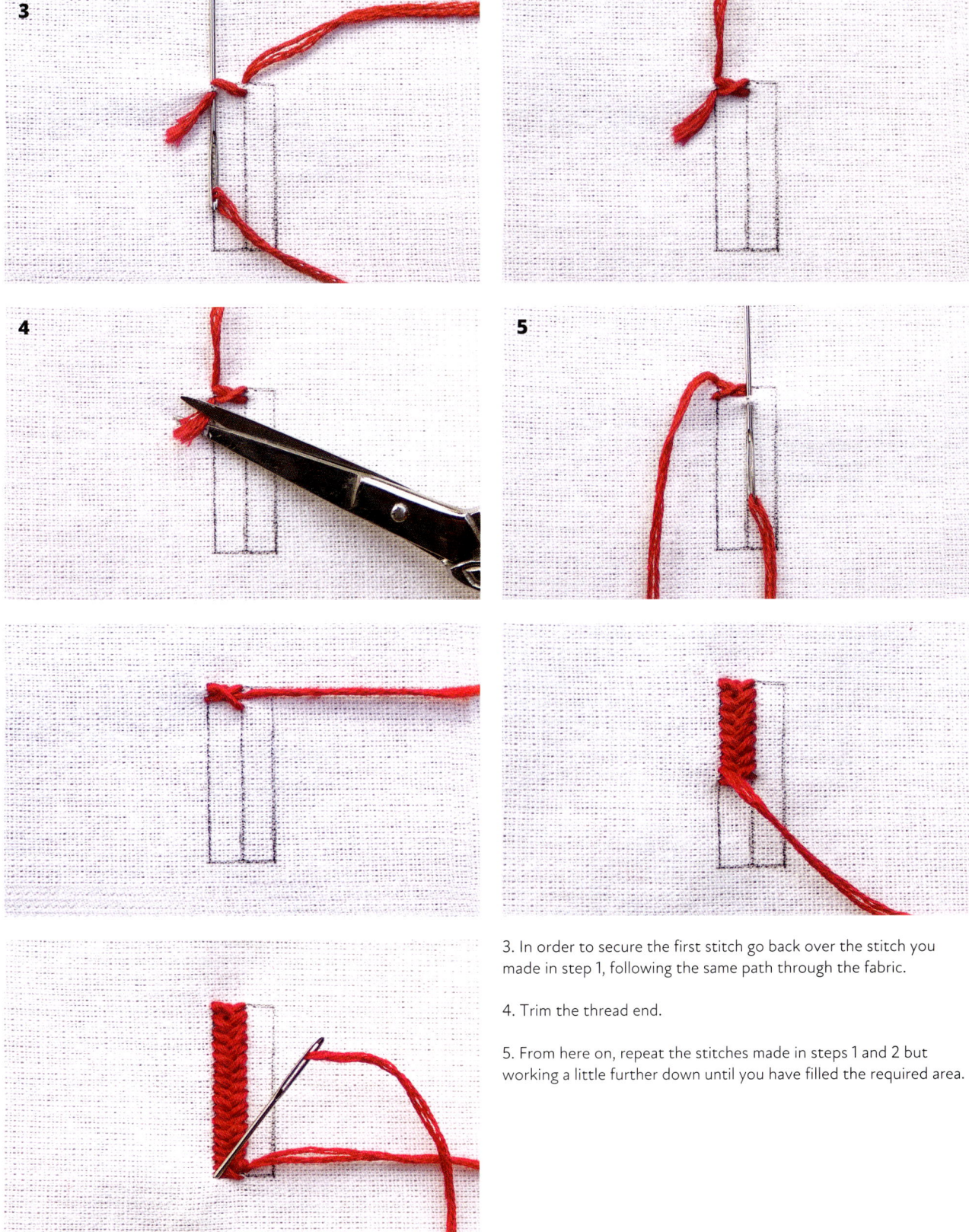

3. In order to secure the first stitch go back over the stitch you made in step 1, following the same path through the fabric.

4. Trim the thread end.

5. From here on, repeat the stitches made in steps 1 and 2 but working a little further down until you have filled the required area.

To finish
The same type of finish is used for all stitches.
  Go through the fabric and on the reverse you will find a dotted line of tiny stitches.
  Weave the thread through three of these tiny stitches and trim the end flush with the fabric.

To embroider adjacent strips you can use the previous stitches as references to keep your stitches even.

When using this stitch as a filling stitch, the work may be monochrome or multicoloured, changing thread for each strip. It is very intuitive embroidery, as the stitching fits the shape to be filled. You can divide the shape into strips with a pencil or fabric marker to use as a guide.

A finished embroidery from the back.

The same embroidery from the front.

Backstitch

This stitch is very common and appears in many types of embroidery in the world. Although we call it backstitch here, elsewhere it is known as stem stitch. It is used for the linear parts of Tenango embroidery.

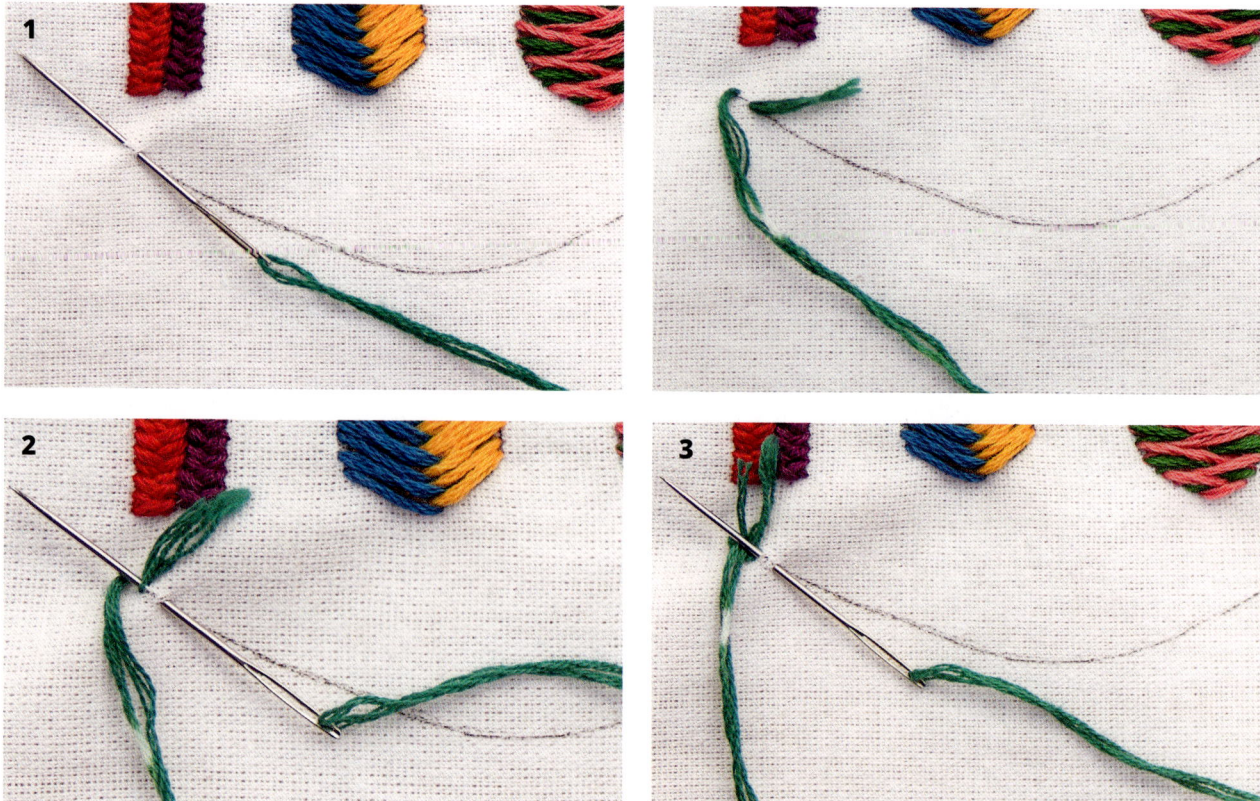

1. Start at the top of the fabric. Begin half a stitch length from the start of the stitching line and take a small stitch back to the start. Pull through, leaving a short thread end.

2. With the working thread to one side, take a small stitch back, bringing the needle out at the position of the thread end.

3. Continue in the same way, taking the needle down half a stitch length further on and bringing it out at the end of the previous stitch.

4. After two or three stitches, trim the excess thread.

5. Continue with the rest of the stitching. It is important to take into account the position of the working thread: it does not matter if you leave it above, below, left or right, but you must always keep to the same side.

OVERLEAF
With Tenango embroidery, the pieces look almost as neat on the back (left) as they do on the front (right).

A finished embroidery from the back.

The same embroidery from the front.

Hini
(silent)

Hini is very similar to another embroidery stitch – herringbone stitch – which is also recognized worldwide.

Sadly, the names of the stitches no longer used – *hini* and *xi* (see page 36) – are in Otomi or *hñähñu*, the language spoken in this region which, like the stitches, is in the process of disappearing.

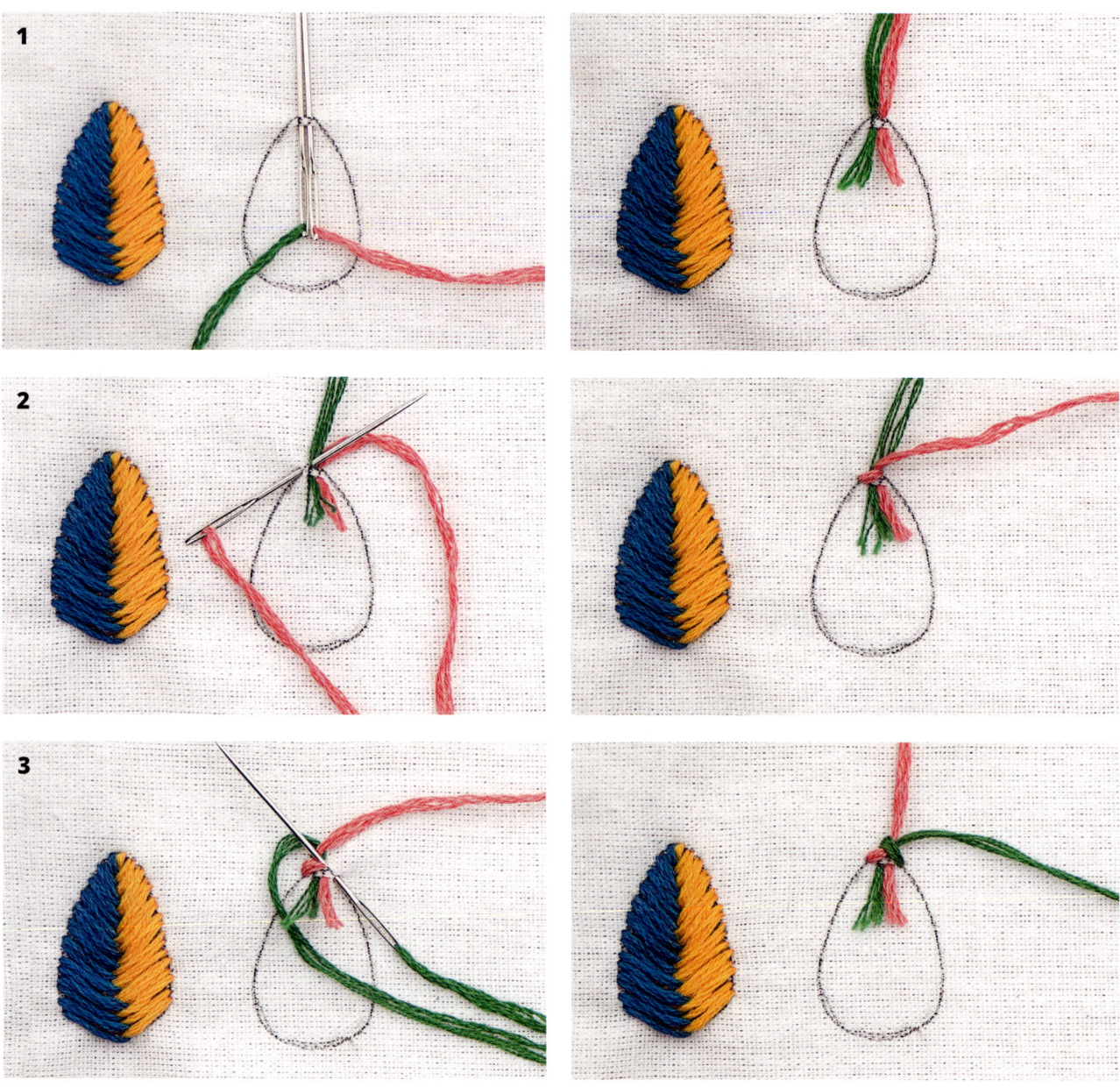

1. With two needles each prepared with its own colour (I have used pink and green threads), make a tiny stitch, bringing both needles out at the centre-top of the shape, leaving short thread tails on the front.

2. With the first colour, pink, cross to one side of the shape and take a small stitch back up to the top of the shape, securing the second colour, green, at the same time.

3. Repeat the step with the second colour (green).

4. Change to the first colour and take a small stitch in the same way on the opposite side of the shape.

5. Change to the second colour and take a small stitch in the same way on the opposite side of the shape again.

6. Continue to infill the shape in the same way.

7. The result will be a uniform interweaving of colours over the shape. Finish off your threads on the back (see page 24).

To find out how to stitch the leaf shape on the left, see pages 36–39.

A finished embroidery from the back.

The same embroidery from the front.

Xi
(tree leaf)

So as not to get lost when working *xi* stitch, it is recommended that you draw additional guidelines on the fabric.

The initial shape is an oval leaf, as for the *hini* stitch. Draw a smaller leaf shape approximately 1mm (1/16in) in from the initial outline. Then divide the shape into three horizontal sections.

1. Start in the same way as for *hini* stitch (see page 32), using two colours.

2. With the second colour (here, yellow), cross the shape and take a small stitch on the far-left of the top horizontal line on the inner outline, this time with the needle pointing going downwards.

3. Repeat the previous step on the other side with the first colour (here, blue).

4. With the second colour, take a small downward-facing stitch close to where the yellow thread first emerged in step 1. Pull gently to anchor the thread.

5. Repeat the previous step with the first colour. Now the two threads should be in the upper part of the leaf shape.

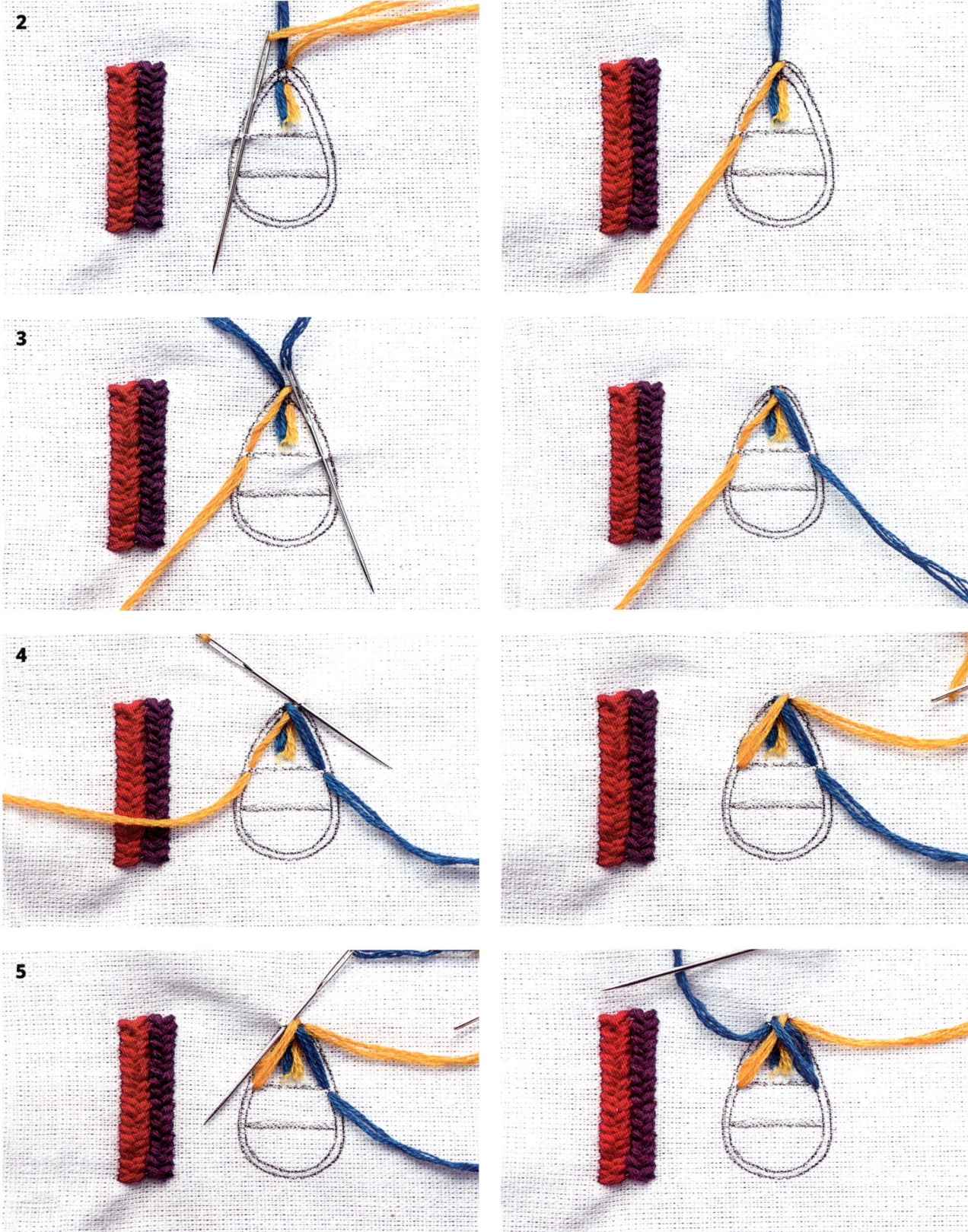

6

7

6. Cross both colours in turn on the diagonal and take a stitch just below the previous one, again on the inner outline. Make sure to alternate the colours as you work.

7. Take the second colour through the top edge as before, this time slightly further down; repeat with the first colour.

8. Carry on embroidering with the two colours in the same way, working downwards. The effect is that the colours change sides and overlap each other.

8. In the end you will have a leaf shape divided into two colours. Finish off on the back (see page 24).

8

9

39

A finished embroidery from the back.

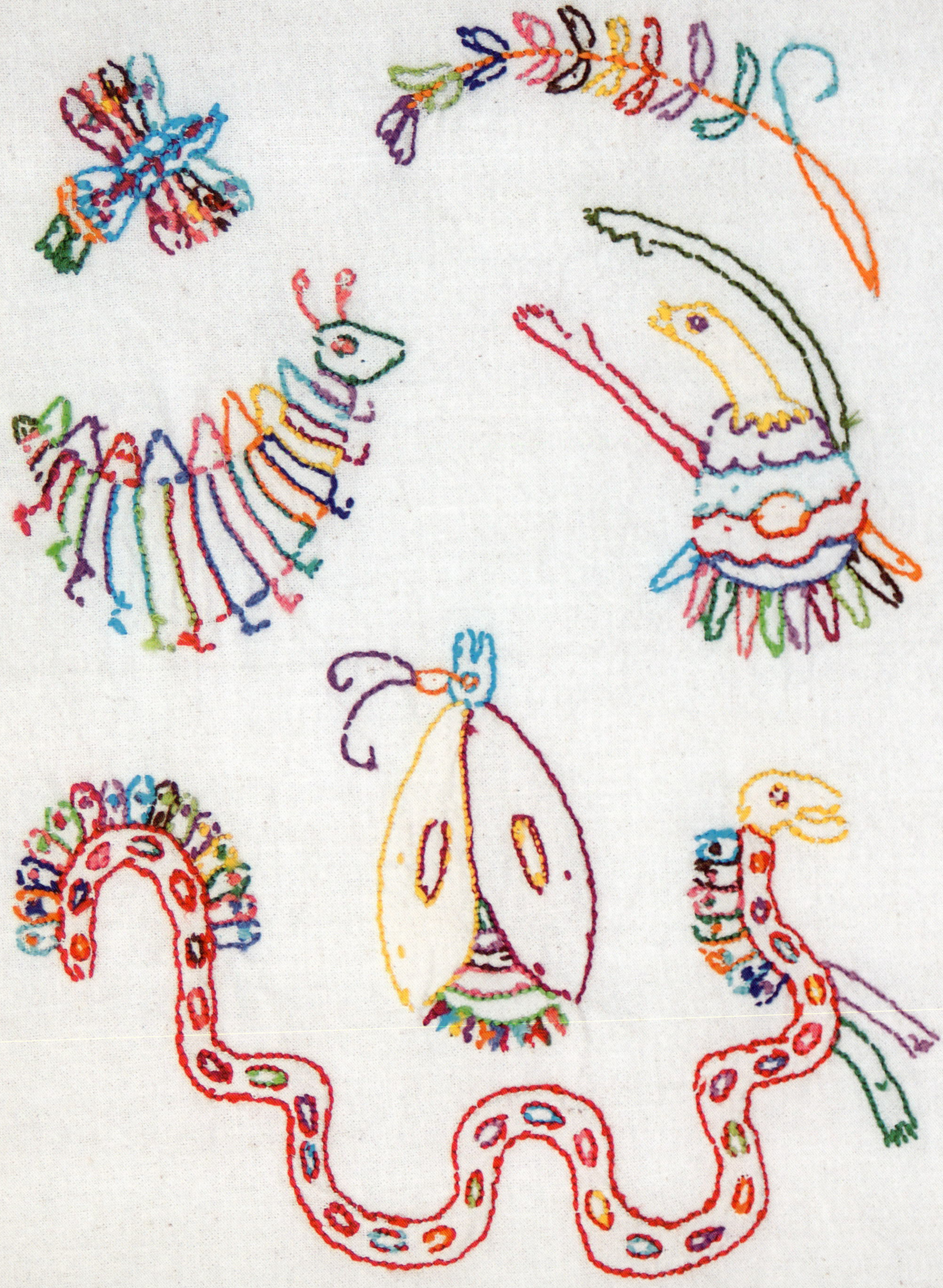

The same embroidery from the front.

Street embroidery

Mexico City

'Packet of green sewing thread over here please!' 'Felt shoes 23 pesos a pair!' 'Not eating lunch in order to buy thread is not wasting time!'

On entering the San Alberto haberdashery, phrases like these are heard all the time.

I was born in Mexico City, a monster of a city that, if you are not careful, eats you up. Here blood and pornography exceed the limits of the newspapers and the streets usually smell of fat from the food. The silence shines because of its absence, the traffic is infernal and there are waves of people going from home to work, firstly all going one way and then all going the other. Depending on the time, I know which side of the street to move to. I know the means of transport, the direction, the time and the right coach so as not to be a victim of urban claustrophobia. Or at least I try to. But embroidery I see with other eyes and, as the city bursts and overflows into visual and olfactory excesses, so does the embroidery, which overflows as it disappears.

The dispersion of cars on the streets, of noise and people crossing rivers of people, was all part of the route for reaching the San Alberto haberdashery, where you can avoid the usual decibels in order to buy hoops and threads and then go for a coffee and embroider with women who, for a change, are twice my age. If Mexico City were to have a traditional embroidery, it would be this. A spectacular embroidery, an embroidery brimming with embroidery.

I developed my street embroidery by combining stitches from *haute couture* with stitches that I learned from the women who embroider coloured napkins in the street of Regina, in the centre of the city. Stitches that were not at all simple, neither the second nor the first.

Lattice work is a type of stitch that is embroidered over itself without having a foundation stitch. With foundation stitches – several appear throughout this book – a base of thread is prepared in the fabric on which another stitch is worked. In lattice work (like woven watermelon stitch on page 62) it is embroidered and then embroidered over.

I use fruit motifs as they are frequently seen on the napkins embroidered by the women. I also like to play and think of this type of work as the exercise of going to the market and selecting fruits that promise juice and flavour from their texture and colour.

Embroidering in the street recaptures the gesture of living in the city, of learning from our environment, appropriating our neighbourhood. To embroider is to live. 'After the earthquake, we thought that there would never be people back here,' said Mrs Amaranta while talking to me about the years the women had spent embroidering there together.

I was away from Mexico for seven months and, on returning, there was no café and there were no women, nor was there any embroidery, in the street. So Pedro (the photographer for this book) and I decided to go to the haberdashery on Correo Mayor and do the route to the café while documenting everything. Except that this time I invited all the people to come and embroider – and they came! It was a way of incentivizing street embroidery and helping it not disappear.

STITCHES
Leaves

For this type of stitch I am using perlé thread no. 5. The thread thickness may vary depending on the scale of the embroidery but perlé is usually used because it gives this type of stitch a voluminous and 'spongy' effect. I am also using both sharp and blunt needles, no. 22. Blunt needles are also called tapestry or upholstery needles.

The stitch is worked on Manta (pure cotton) fabric.

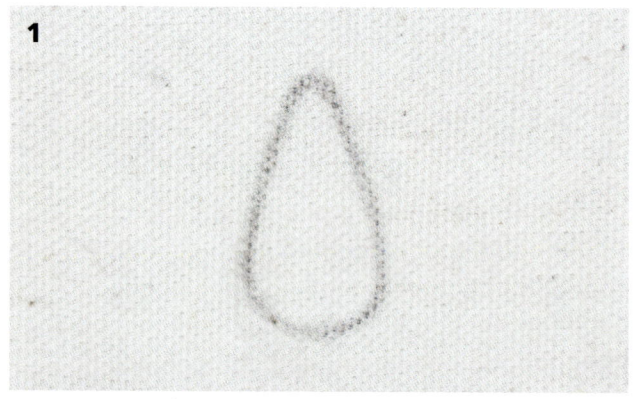
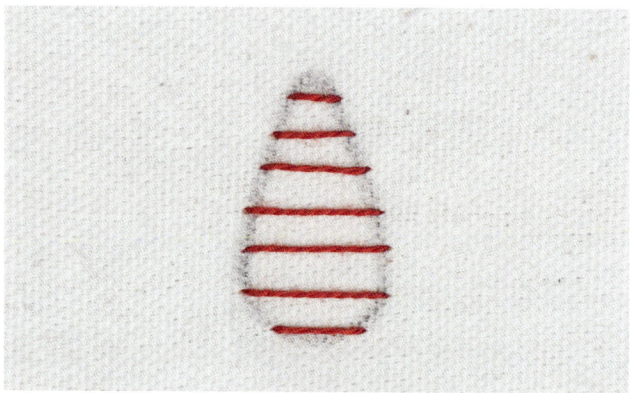
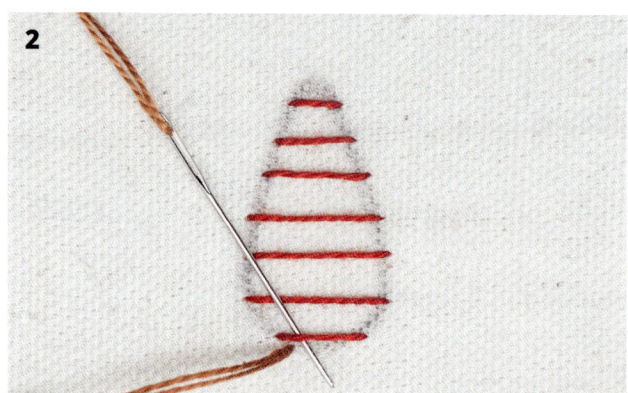

Advice for this stitch: don't put too much pressure on the thread because, if you do, the foundation will move and you will lose the plump form of the stitch. Note that here I have used red thread for the foundation bars so that they show up, but you could use a colour that matches one of the other threads.

1. On a leaf-shaped outline you have to first embroider parallel horizontal lines, as shown in the picture. This thread structure is called a foundation, and the stitch is constructed around it (the needle pierces the fabric only when the stitch requires it). In order to embroider the foundation always use a needle with a point. There are different types of foundations for different types of stitch; as the name suggests, a foundation is an anchor and support for the final embroidery. The base stitches are called foundation stitches and the top stitches are the mounted stitches.

2. With a tapestry needle threaded with a single strand used double, come out at the bottom of the leaf shape and take the needle over and under the first bottom bar of the foundation, then back into the fabric.

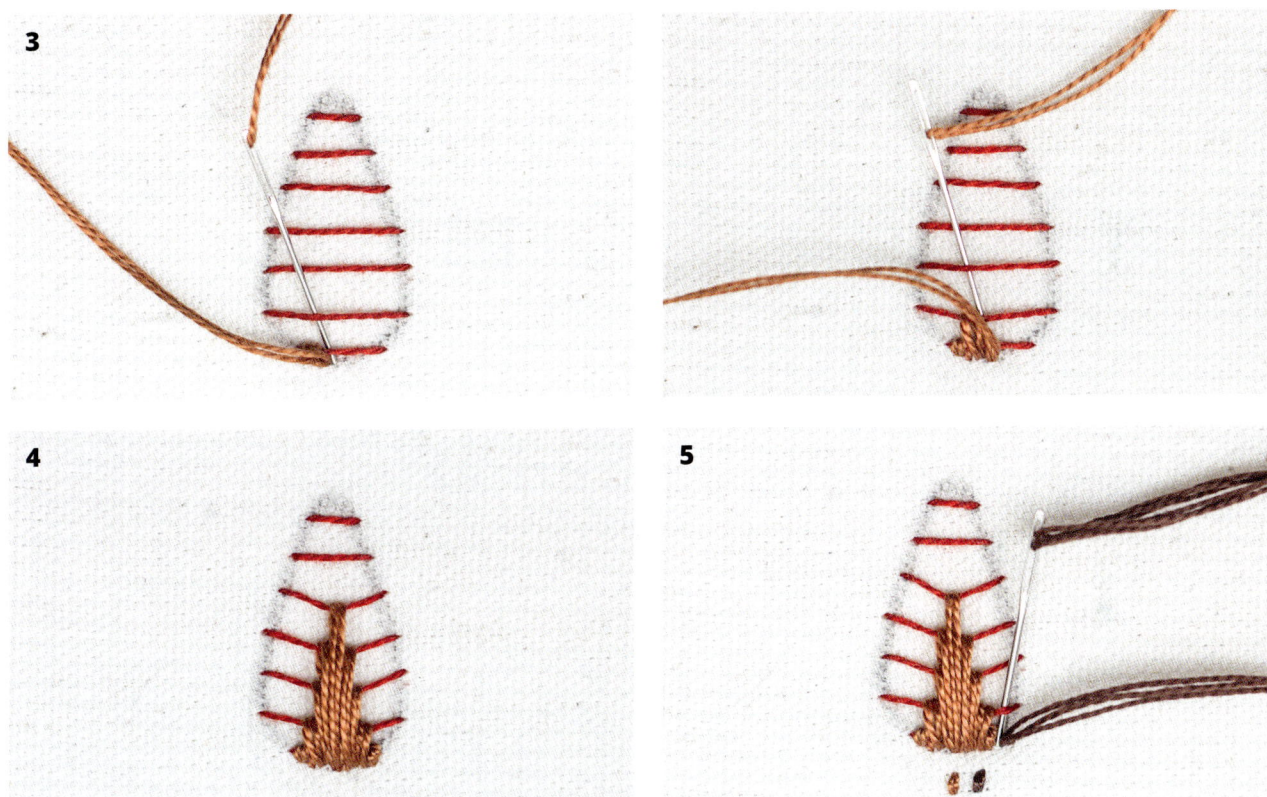

3. Repeat the process for the next stitch along but go up one bar with each stitch, constructing the internal shape of the leaf until you reach the third bar from the top of the foundation stitches.

4. From here do exactly the same but in mirror image, going down one bar with each stitch. Pierce the fabric and finish with a small knot on the reverse.

5. Change colour in the needle but this time with two strands (doubled) in order to make the external part of the petal bulkier. Come out to the right of the far-right stitch in the first colour, on the bottom edge of the outline, then weave the needle under the second bar of the foundation. Pass through the fabric on the leaf, coming out close to where you went in. Skip over the bottom bar of the foundation and go over and under the second bar, as shown.

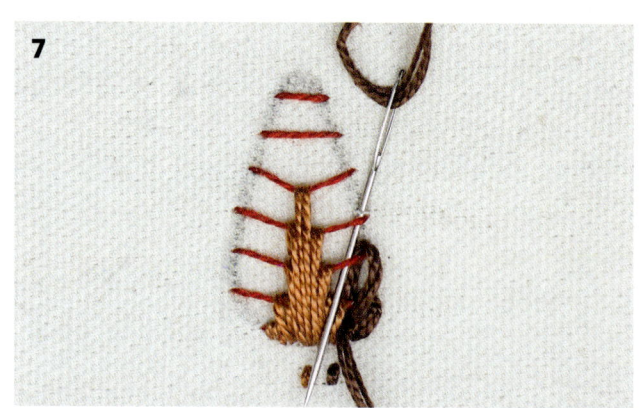
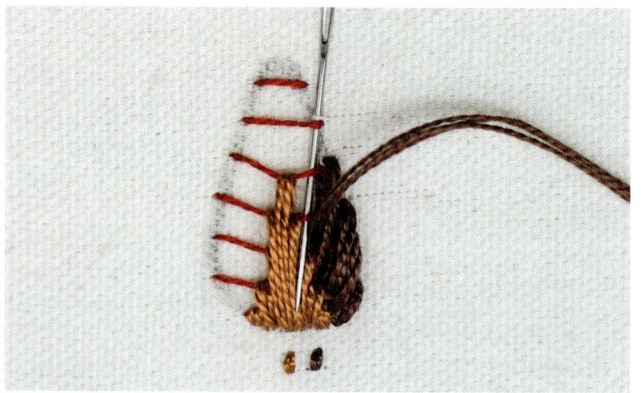

6. Go up one bar of the foundation, skipping over the bottom bar, and go over and then under the third and second bars, working towards the centre. Anchor the stitch in the same way as in the previous step.

7. Continue in the same way, moving up one bar with each stitch, going under two bars at a time, until you reach the top of the shape. Then finish with a small knot on the reverse when you anchor the last stitch.

8. Repeat on the left side, starting again from the bottom of the leaf. It is better to finish and restart from this edge so that the direction of the stitches forms a mirror image.

Open banana

It is preferable to use this stitch, which is a widely-spaced version of cretan open filling stitch, when the motif to be worked lends itself to sub-division into bars or lines. Note that the outline doubles as a foundation stitch for the filling – you have to define the shape of the figure to be infilled using reverse chain stitch.

This stitch is worked on a cotton fabric, using a Sharps no. 22 needle for the outline, a blunt needle for the infilling, and a single strand of size 5 perlé thread.

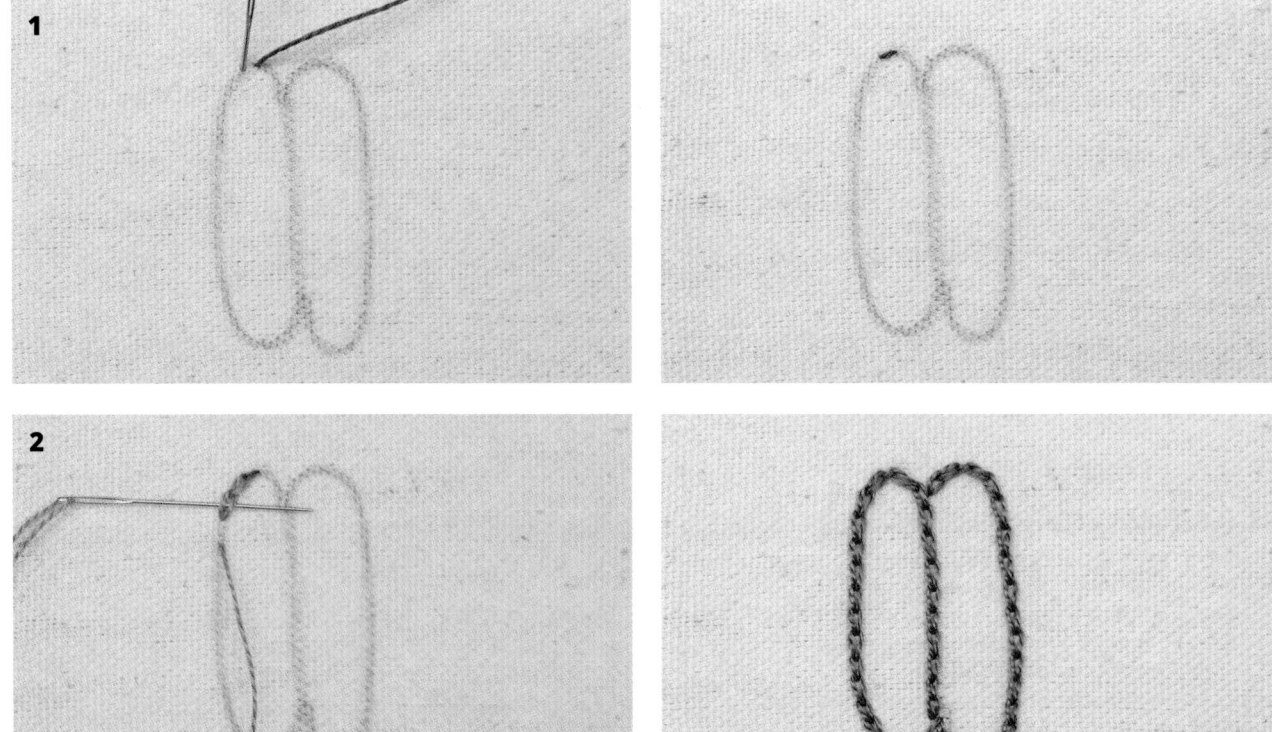

1. Make a small straight stitch on the outline of your shape as shown: this will act as the anchor for the first chain at the top of the shape. Bring the needle out a stitch length farther along, weave it under the straight stitch then take the needle down through the fabric back in through the hole where the thread first emerged. Pull gently so the loop lies flat. Do not put too much pressure on the stitch – if you do, the chain will close and the effect will be lost.

2. Come out a stitch-length away, weave the needle under the loops of the previous chain stitch, then take it down where the needle emerged. Continue in this way to complete the outline. Ensure that the whole outline is uniform, with chains of the same size, and, as far as possible, with the same number of chains on each side of the shape to be infilled – this will keep the filling even.

3. With two strands of another colour threaded into a blunt needle, come out inside the first chain of your foundation stitch.

4. Cross over and pick up only the internal side of the opposite chain, keeping the working thread below the needle as you pull the needle through; do not pierce the fabric.

5. Cross over and pick up the next chain in the same way.

6. Continue in this way until you have filled the shape.

Change colour if you wish, but it is important to continue working with a blunt/tapestry needle. Come out again through the first chain, jump the first line and, from the second, start to pick up the chains together until you reach the base of the stitch.

Secure the thread by passing through the fabric and come out in the next chain. Repeat from step 4 into the chains you have already made.

You can use as many colours as you wish. As a result you will have a highly ornamental raised stitch, which is very simple to do.

Pineapple for the girl[1]

This intricate filling starts with a background of straight satin stitches over which we work a vertical trellis followed by a diagonal one. The whole thing is then further secured and embellished – the perfect filling for a pineapple.

This stitch is worked on a cotton fabric, using a no. 22 Sharps needle, and a single strand of size 5 perlé thread.

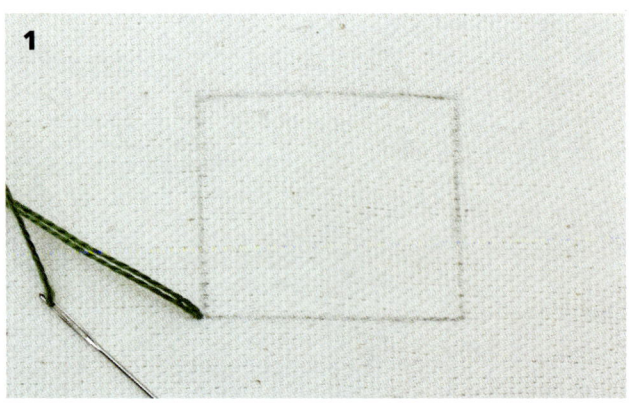

1. Start infilling the area with long satin stitches first. Come out with a doubled strand of thread on the outline of the shape and go in on the other side.

2. Come out very close to where you entered and stitch to the opposite side until the whole of the shape is infilled. This stitch is called *medio satín* in Mexico.

3. Finish as on page 24.

[1] The original name of this stitch, *Piña para la niña*, is a traditional Mexican saying, meaning 'give the girl some sweets', which sadly does not translate as poetically into English!

4. Once infilled, use a new colour and one strand of thread to work evenly spaced lines over the satin stitch, perpendicular to the infill. The spacing will depend on the size of the shape being filled.

5. Now work another set of lines at right angles to the first set with the same spacing, and still using one strand of thread, to create a grid.

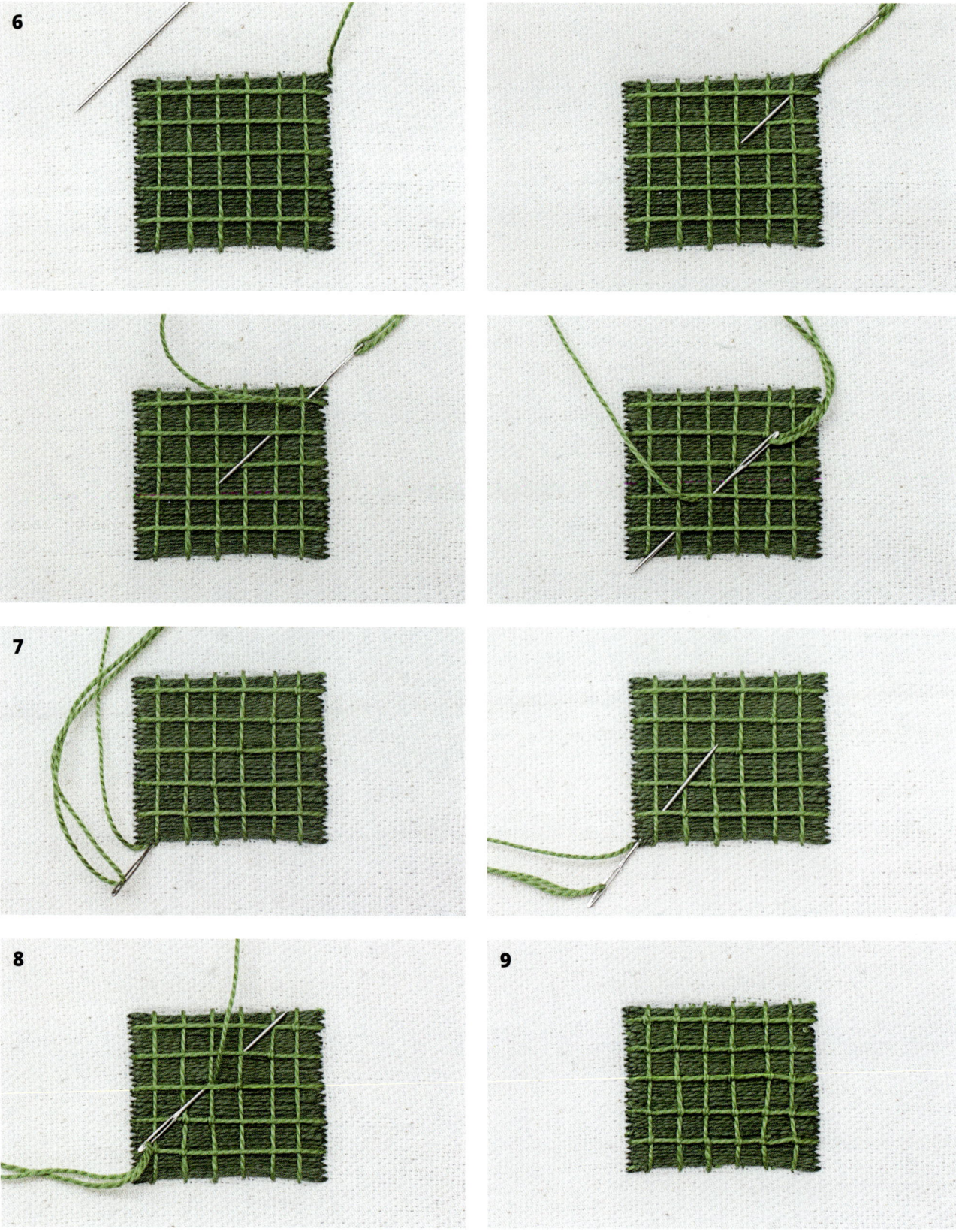

6. Turn the fabric 45 degrees so that you can see the embroidery as if it were a diamond, and in this way it is easier for you to complete this step. (The photographs have not been turned to make it easier for you to follow.) With the same second colour and a single strand of thread, come out at one corner of the shape. Then, without piercing the fabric, go below the initial infill, bringing the needle out just on the far side of the first grid intersection. Take the needle down before the same intersection to create an anchor, under the infill and out just beyond the next intersection of the grid. Continue in the same way to secure the intersections. Do not pull these stitches too tightly as you will need to thread the needle through them later.

7. After the final intersection, go under the infill to the edge and take a small stitch to secure the thread, then turn and work back across the grid in the same way along the next diagonal of intersections.

8. Continue in this way to complete the line, pierce the fabric at the end and come out on the next line.

9. Secure the whole of the grid in this way. This is your A grid.

10. Change to a single thread of a third colour. Starting at any corner, pass the needle through the securing stitches in a diagonal line across the grid.

11. Repeat this step for the whole grid.

12. Repeat steps 10 and 11 but at right angles to create a B grid over the initial grid.

13. Change thread colour and come out on one side of the work.

14. Take a small stitch to secure the thread, then pass the needle under the infill and bring it out at the intersection where you want your flower to be.

15. From here, work around the intersection in the same way as when working a whipped wheel: go under the first 'spoke', back to the start of the last stitch, then under the first and second spokes; then go back over one spoke and forward under two until you have created a small flower.

16. You can do as many turns as you wish in order to make the motif larger or smaller.

17. Finish on the reverse as usual (see page 24).

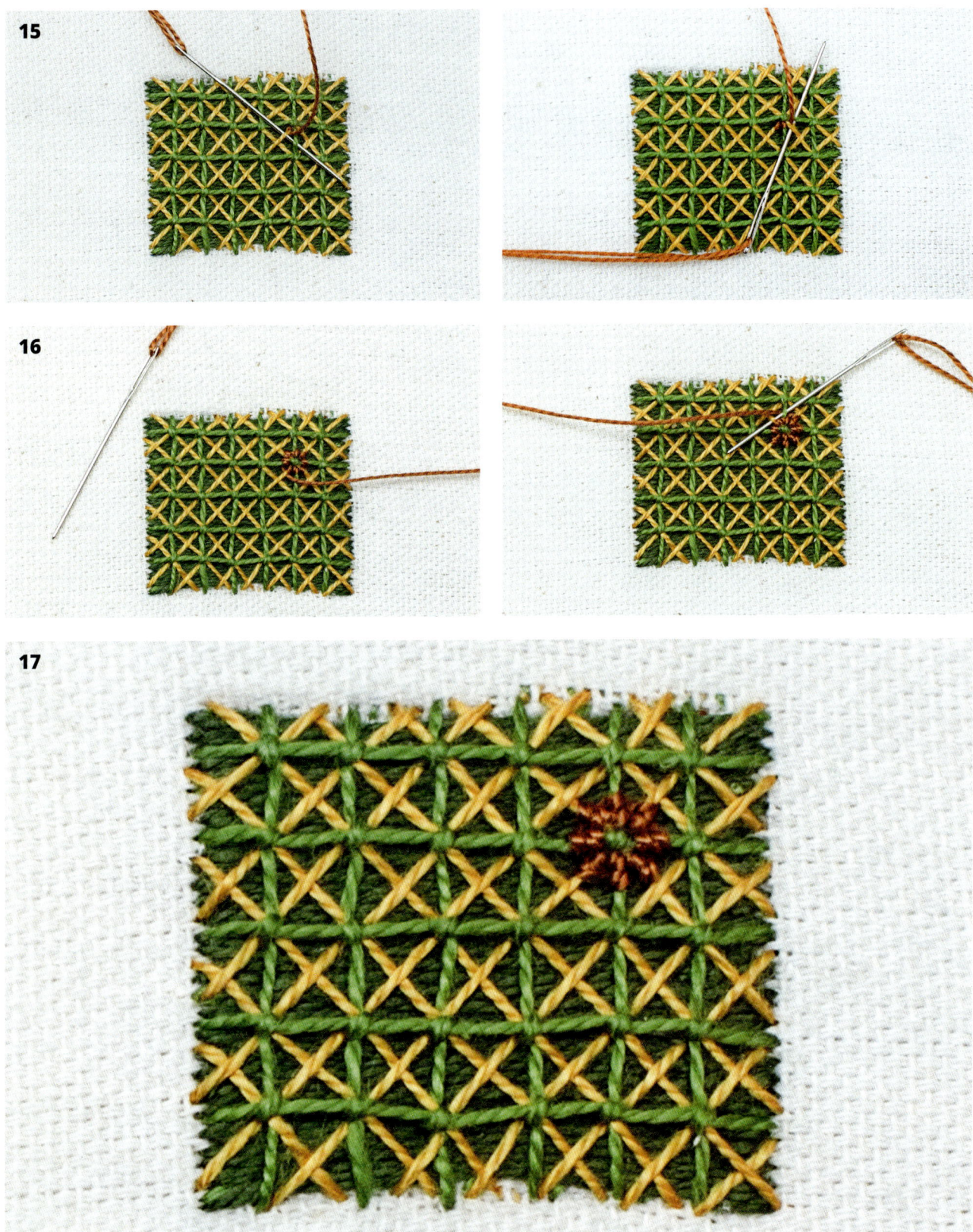

A finished embroidery from the back.

The same embroidery from the front.

Woven watermelon

Choose two colours of thread as a minimum in order to add contrast to the stitch and so that it stands out. You can do this in a single colour, but you will have a uniform infill with a subtle texture.

This stitch is worked on a cotton fabric, using a no. 22 Sharps needle, and a single strand of size 5 perlé thread.

1. With a single strand of thread embroider satin stitch in two colours, working in multiples of five stitches in each colour before switching colour again.

2. Change orientation; this time the stitch should weave horizontally across the satin stitches. Still using a single thread, select five strands and lift them with the needle in order to pass the thread behind them; you have to count five and go over, then count five and go under. This work is called weaving or surface darning and in this case goes over or under five stitches at a time. Work a total of five horizontal stitches, all going over or under the same satin stitches. Then switch colour, and work a set of five satin stitches all going over the stitches you went under in the first set and going under the ones you went over.

3. In the end you will have a weave that looks great in a mix of colours. If you want to give it a bit more contrast, you can use another colour and pass threads randomly to enhance your work (see the images on pages 64 and 71).

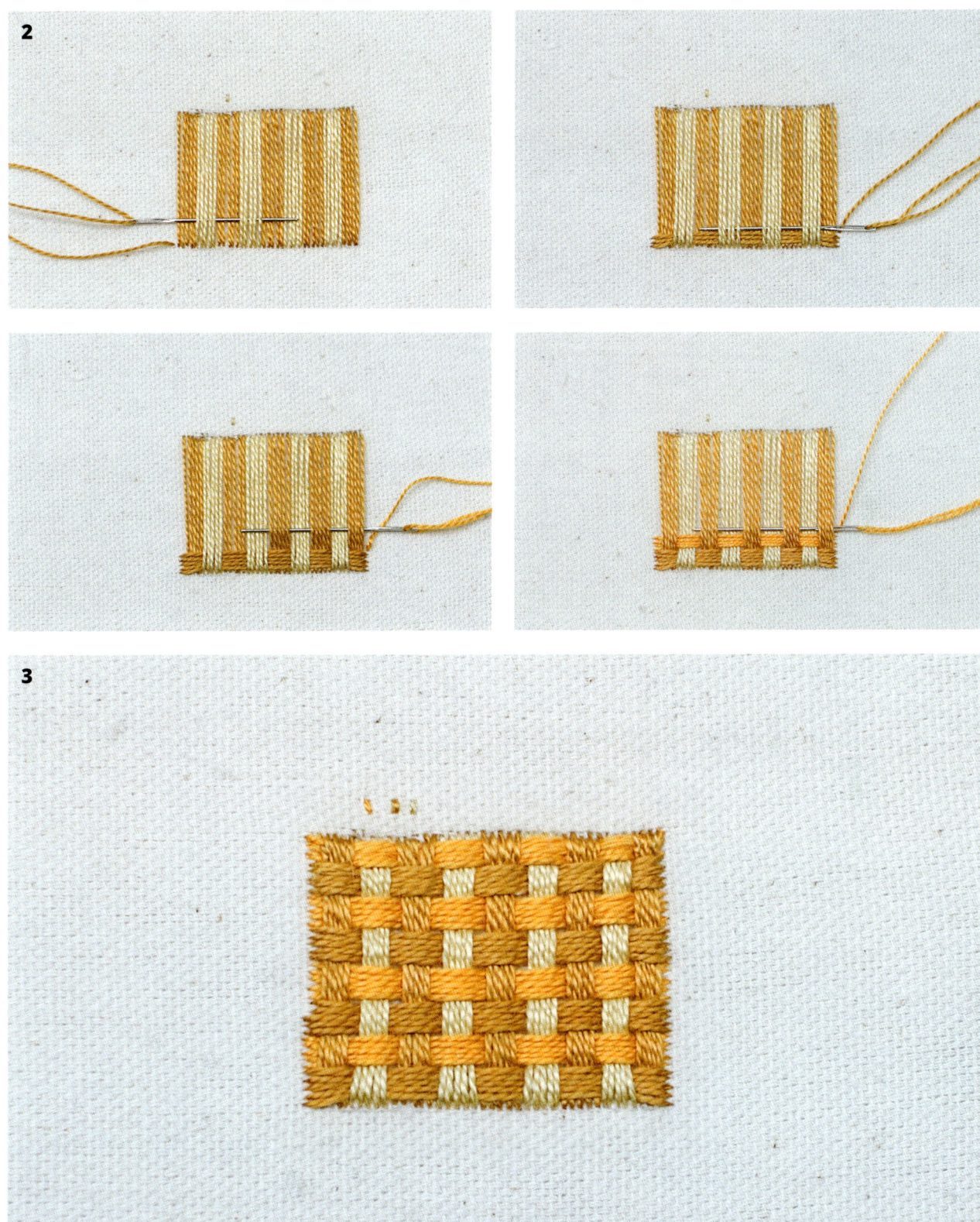

Strawberry

When you work this stitch with colours from the same family, an optical effect is created that blends the colours harmoniously (see the strawberry on page 71). I have deliberately used contrasting colours in this sample so that the stitches stand out.

This stitch is worked on a cotton fabric, using both a no. 22 Sharps and blunt needle, and a single strand of size 5 perlé thread.

1. Start by working satin stitch over the area to be covered (see steps 1–3 on page 54).

2. With another colour, embroider a uniform grid over this and secure it as in the first pineapple grid (see steps 4–9 on pages 55–57).

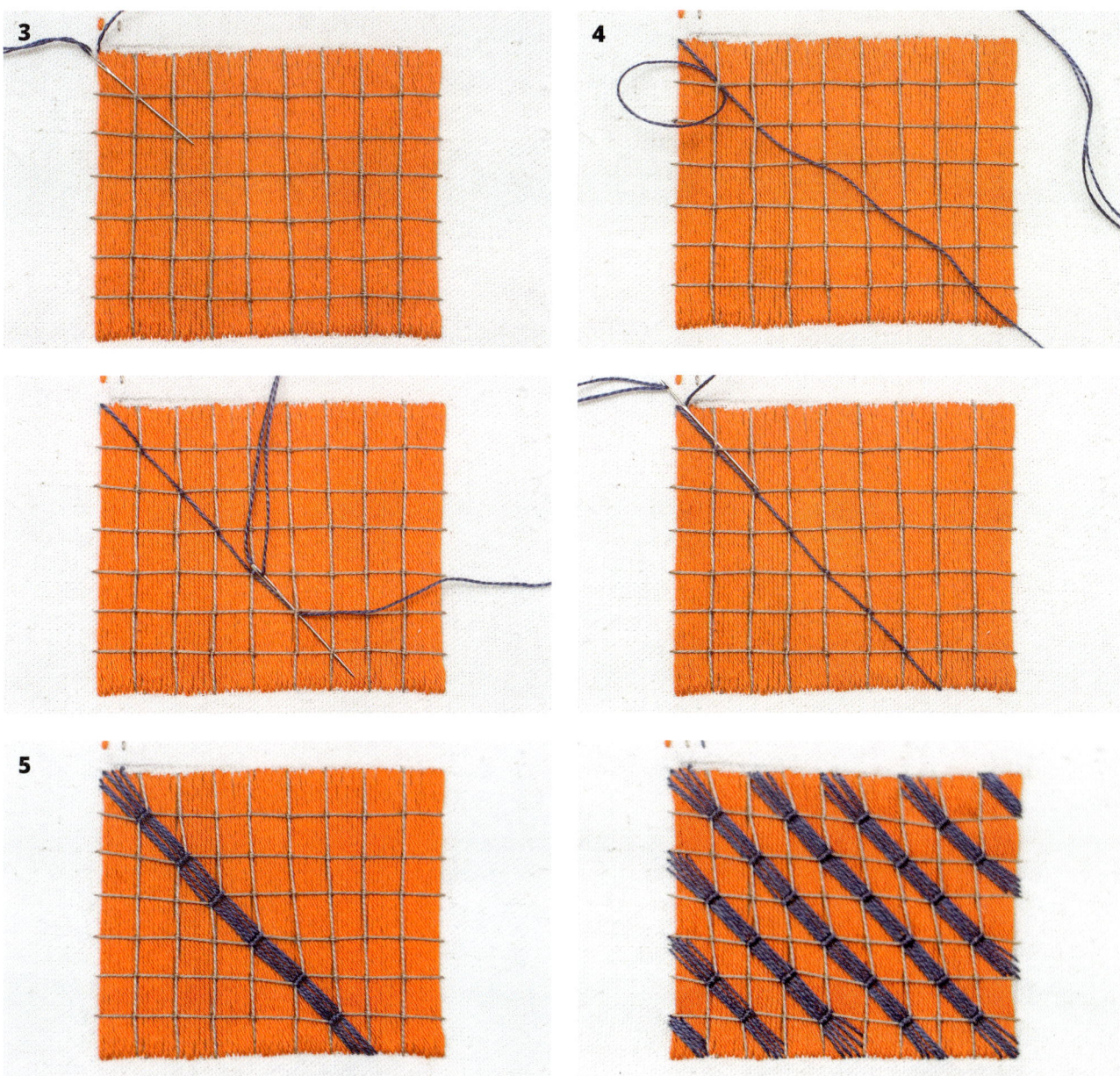

3. We are going to work on the diagonals created by the grid. You may like to rotate the fabric a little in order to see it better. With a third colour (violet), bring your needle out at the top-left corner of the shape.

4. With this colour, pick up the lines that intersect in the direction of the diagonal: take the needle under and out after the first intersection, back under that intersection and out after the second intersection and then repeat the process to the end (similar to step 6 on page 56).

5. Repeat, working over the same intersections until you have a group of five threads. Repeat to cover the whole area of the shape.

6

7

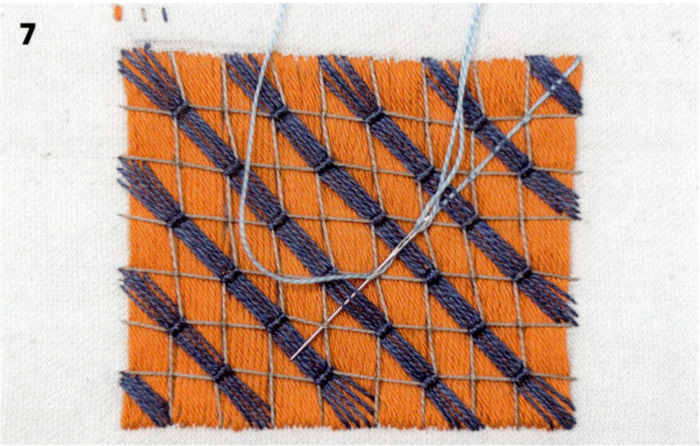

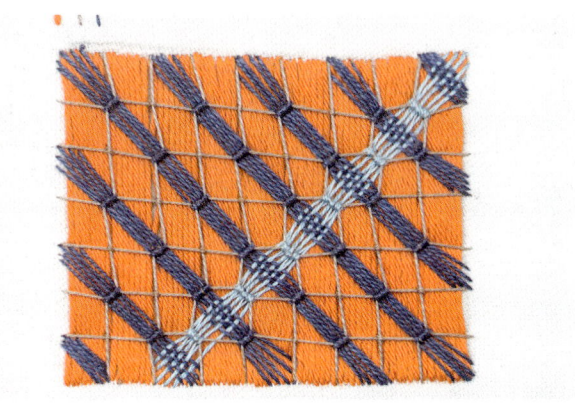

8

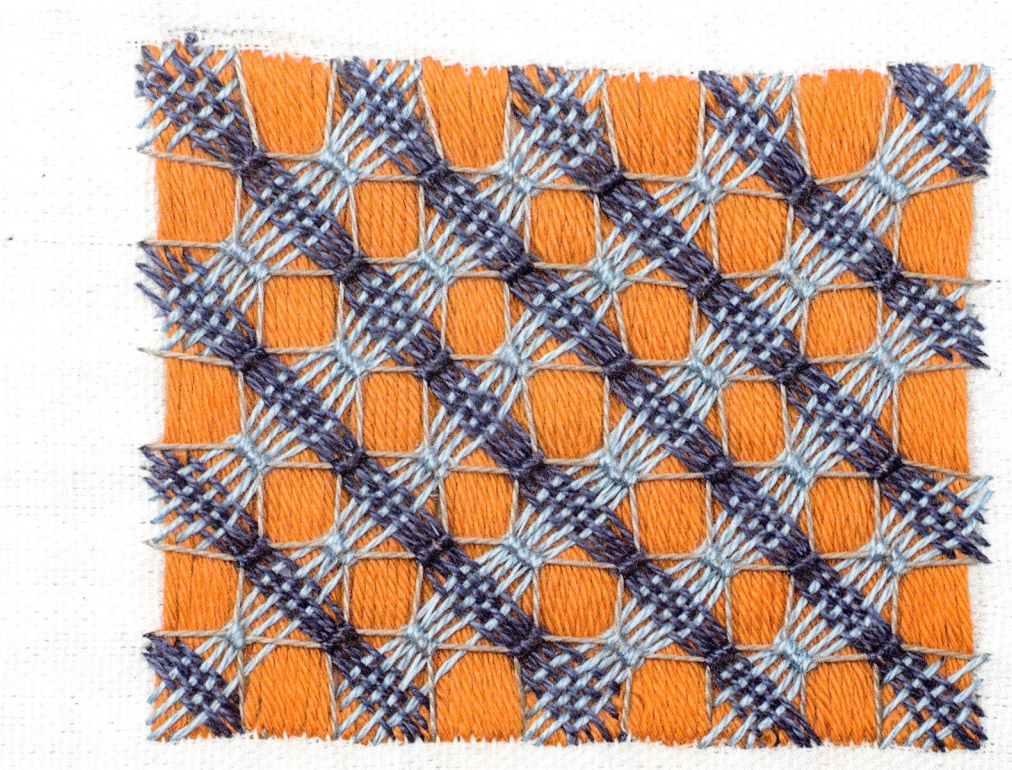

6. Now, with a fourth colour, you have to infill the rest of the shape. Weave groups of five threads on the diagonal as in steps 3 and 4, this time working in the opposite direction. Bring your needle out at the top right-hand corner.

7. Pick up the grid intersections in the same way as in step 4 but, this time, when you reach each set of five diagonal threads you should weave through them, going under the first thread, over the second, and so on, and doing the opposite on the second pass.

8. The grid will open up with the natural tension of the weaving and rounded sections will remain in the finished work.

This stitch can also be seen applied to the watermelon embroidery shown on pages 64–65.

A finished embroidery from the back.

The same embroidery from the front.

Mazahua embroidery

Valle de Bravo, Mexico state

'Mazahua embroidery requires understanding basic geometry and mathematics, using reasoning and having a passion for perfection.'

Jan Cristian, embroiderer.

In Valle de Bravo, the spectacle of Mazahuan women with their coloured plates and their embroidery hidden under their petticoats is a beautiful one. It is curious, then, that this time, the person who taught me to embroider was a man. A lad of 21 years, Jan was audaciously young for the skill that he had at his hands.

It is said that Mazahua embroidery has to contain mistakes because the only thing that is perfect is God. And boy did I make them – although I was not permitted to make any. 'Make the thread one with the fabric', Jan told me, while I had my head full of frustration, with the sensation of someone trying to learn the seven times table and failing.

Mazahua embroidery has a visual logic to learning the steps, but it is not a dance. It is a march, a waving flag. It is to let yourself be taken over by time. For the Mazahua woman, embroidery has always been a form of writing. I do not speak the language, although always, when I undertake the task of learning a new type of embroidery, I think beyond the embroidery, to everything that happens while embroidering and how the language is a fundamental part of understanding it. How to feel in a language that you do not understand? How to feel in a way in which almost nobody wants to speak? I do not allow myself to approach the work before learning the Mazahua words that, for me, are basic, such as 'good morning' (*jiasma*), goodnight (*tsökuaji*) and 'thank you' (*pokjú*).

It is fascinating how people who work with their hands are usually more accessible. And I say 'accessible' to give an adjective to the recurrent reaction – in indigenous communities – of suspicious and disapproving looks aimed at anyone who steps in there for the first time.

I always arrive with my guard down, as my mission is not war. Mine is hidden darning. Accustomed to not believing in the good intentions of others and to receiving gifts in exchange for their work, Mazahuans not involved in artisan production openly mistrust those arriving in their community. Needless to say, my curiosity has not always been welcome.

People are not easy. But in the awkwardness with 'this strange girl' I see a bastion of historic and cultural resistance to which it is an honour to give way in order to enter. I tried to show respect with distance, as they showed from the start.

There are two important Mazahuan settlements: one in Michoacán and the other in Mexico state. In both they do cross stitch with two needles, wool on wool, but only in one community of San Felipe Santiago (in Mexico state) do they do fine embroidery of cotton on cotton. In Mexico state you cannot get good quality wool because of the altitude and the temperature. As a result this type of embroidery is worked in cotton.

In the symbolism of Mazahuan embroidery we can find not only the natural elements but also that which could be the myth of the creation of the Deer People. The technique and the motifs have been passed from mouth to mouth for generations.

It is difficult to get an idea of Mazahuan origin stories as the archive of its culture is practically non-existent. For this reason we have to find its history elsewhere. In Mazahuan embroidery we have a perfect concept of the structure of a drawing. The stitch, the line, the outline, the direction, the tone, the colour, the texture, the size, the scale and the movement are elements that mean the Mazahua embroidery has a very specific logic. It is an elemental thought that is not present in other types of Mexican embroidery.

For the Mazahuan community embroidery has been a way of being maintained in time, of an enduring existence, to ensure that their presence in the world does not go unnoticed.

A young widow does not wear colour because in mourning bright colours are not worn: 'One gets tired of seeing but one stops crying'. And embroidery does precisely this – makes the eye tired from labour but distracts the soul from mourning.

Before I go I promise to return to give them a book in which their stories appear. It doesn't really matter to them. I say goodbye as affectionately as my clumsy Mazahua and my face allow me to: '*Ndo nichko ra jogútsui*', which means 'You will soon be better', although I thought it meant 'See you soon'. Now, thinking about it, it seems logical, like embroidery.

STITCHES
Two-needle cross stitch: straight line

The Mazahuan people call it 'two-needle embroidery' but it is worked with only one needle. What they call 'needles' are in fact the threads of the weft and the warp of the fabric on which they are embroidering.

In Mazahua embroidery knots are never used.

The stitches throughout this chapter are worked on aida/openweave fabric, using a blunt no. 22 needle, and a single strand of mouliné thread – although it is easier to work these stitches with one strand of size 8 perlé thread.

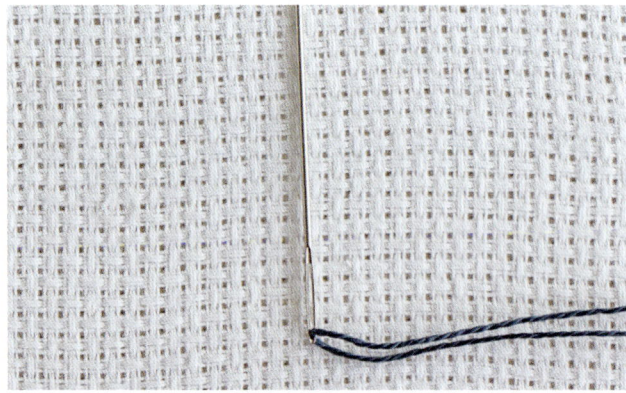

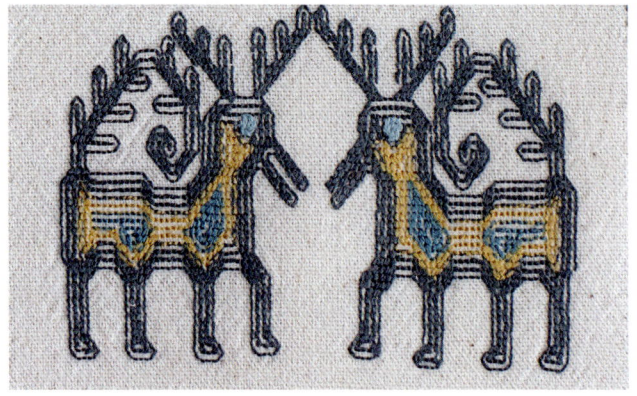

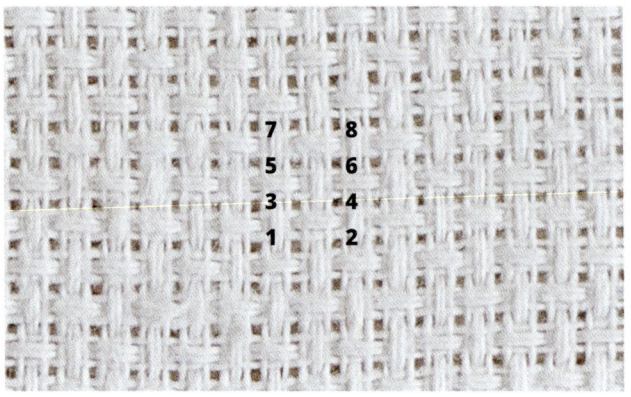

In order to do the stitches I will use a tapestry needle with perlé thread on aida fabric so that it is simpler to follow; the stitches are usually made with one strand of mouliné thread on a cotton fabric. In Mazahua embroidery knots are never used.

I have numbered the holes in the aida fabric so that you know exactly where to place the needle.

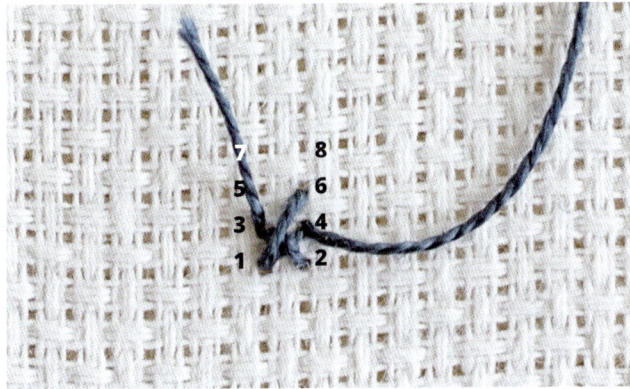

1. Start at 3 at the top of the fabric, leaving a tail and coming out at 1.

2. Cross over, entering at 4 and coming out at 2.

3. Form a cross, securing the thread end at the same time, entering again at 3 and leaving at 1.

4. From 1 enter at 6. Here is where the overstitch is made which gives it the name two-needle cross stitch, as it gives the impression that it is done with two needles because of the over-embroidery. Come out at 4.

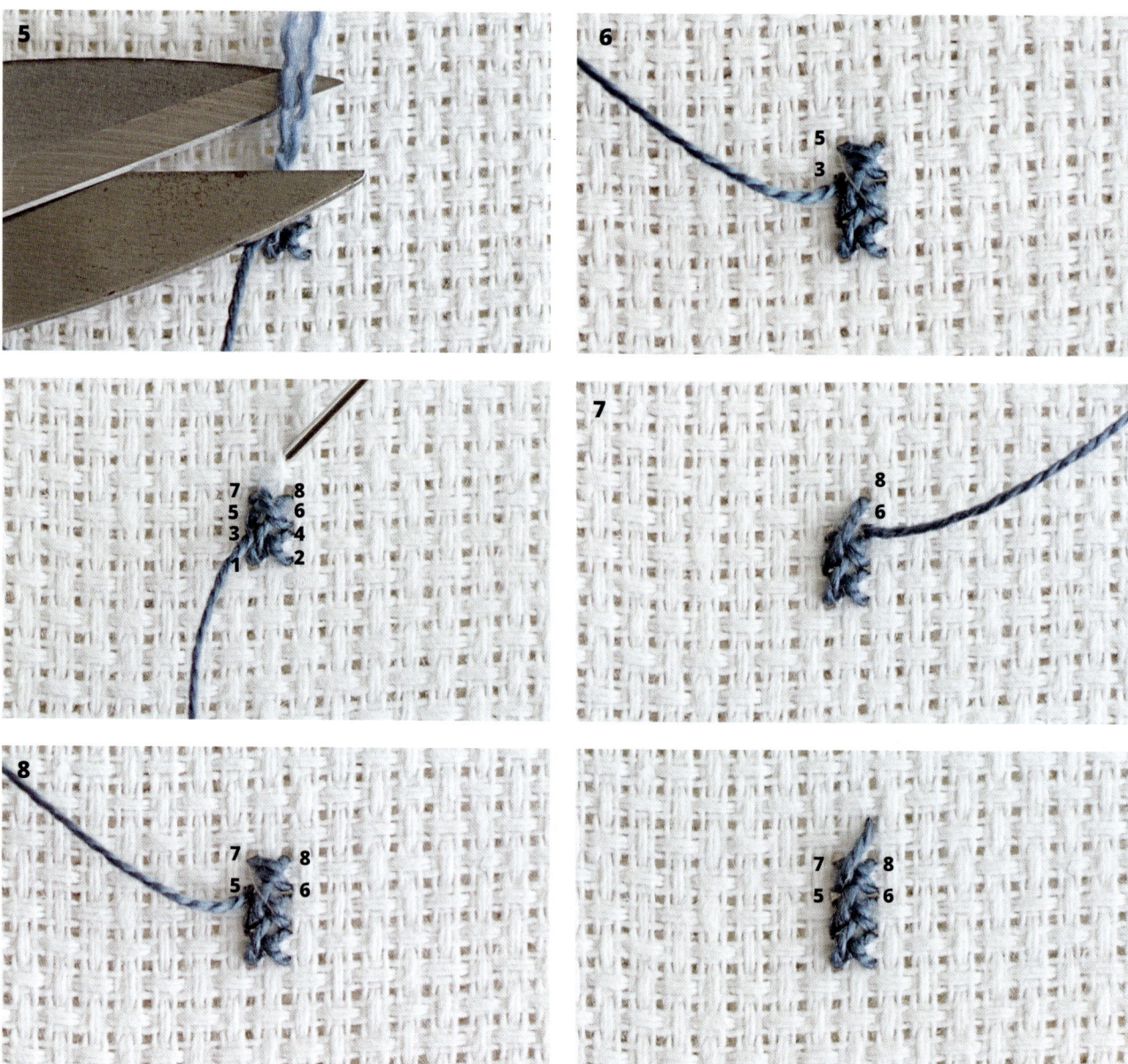

5. You can now trim off the initial tail. Ideally hide it in the cross stitch so that the embroidery remains firm.

6. Go in at 5 and come out at 3.

7. Here the cross from the beginning is formed again, where the long stitch comes out to form the two-needle cross stitch, entering at 8. Come out at 6.

8. Go in at 7 to create the base cross again and come out at 5 ready to start the long stitch.

9. Continue like this to complete the section of line that you want.

10. If the stitch is worked correctly, you should see a pair of parallel lines on the back of the work.

9

10

A finished embroidery from the back.

The same embroidery from the front.

Two-needle cross stitch: turning diagonally to the left

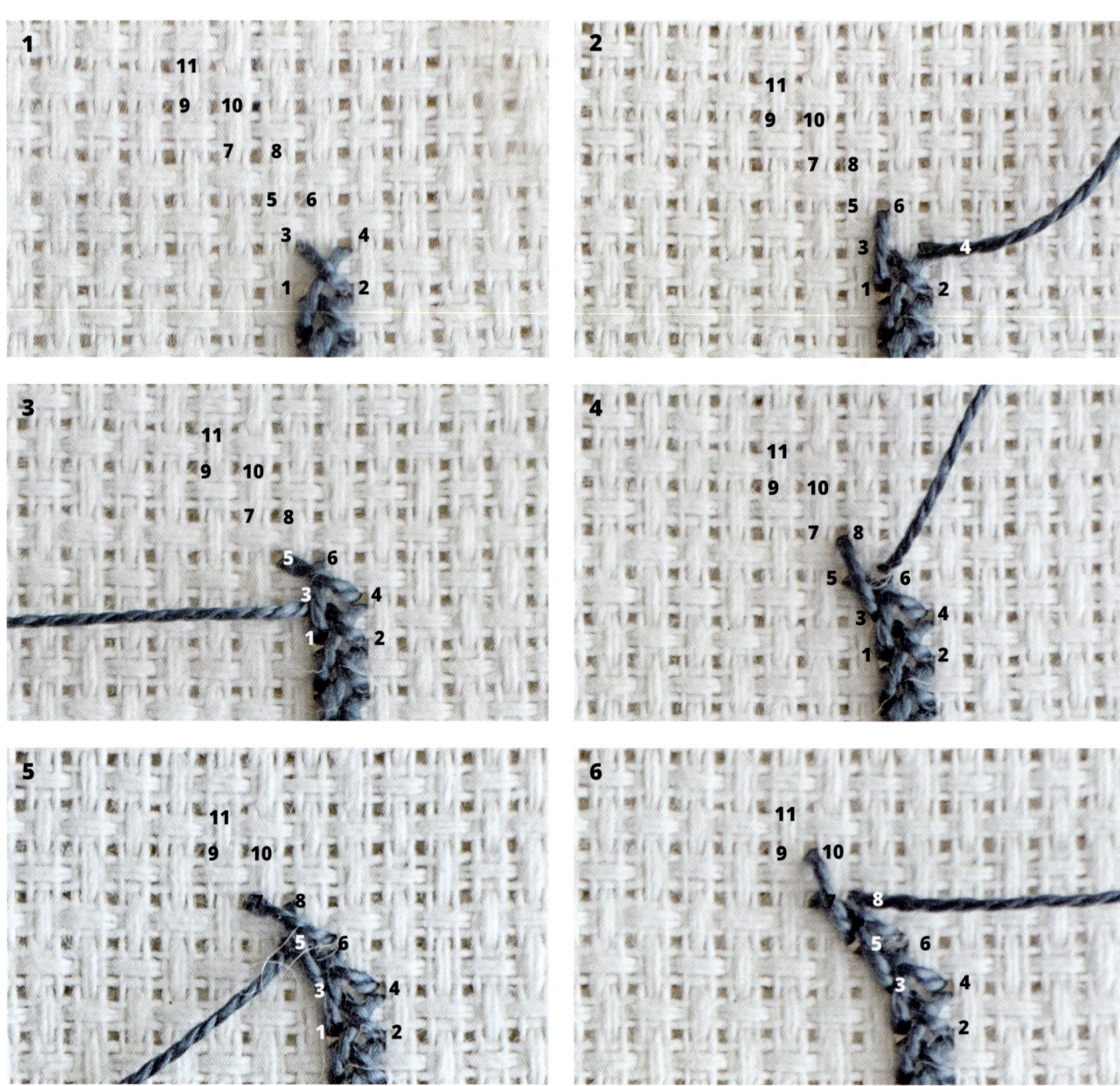

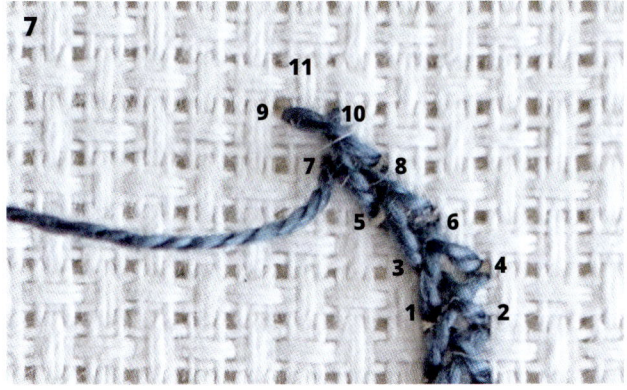

1. To turn diagonally, I am going to start just before the long stitch; in other words, after step 3 on page 75. To do this I have again numbered the holes in the aida, this time in order to explain the diagonal.

2. Picking up at step 3 (page 75), the thread should be emerging at 1 about to start the cross stitch. Go in at 6, two holes directly above, and cross behind to come out at 4.

3. Enter at 5 and come out at 3.

4. Enter at 8 and come out at 6.

5. Enter at 7 and come out at 5.

6. Enter at 10 and come out at 8.

7. Enter at 9 and come out at 7.

8. Enter at 11 and come out at 10. If you look at the diagonal, these are just long stitches interlaced.

9. Continue like this to the end of the required section.

10. To finish, pass the needle under the braid and cut off the excess carefully. Look at the back of the fabric – there should be parallel lines.

Two-needle cross stitch: turning diagonally to the right

1. Just as for the diagonal double-laid cross stitch line on pages 80–81, you have to start from the same point, before doing the long stitch, at step 3 on page 75.

2. Picking up again at step 3 of the two-needle cross stitch straight line (page 75), the thread should be emerging at 1 ready to start the cross. Enter at 5 and cross behind to come out at 3.

3. Enter at 6 and come out at 4.

4. Enter at 7 and come out at 5.

5. Enter at 8 and come out at 6.

6. Enter at 9 and come out at 7.

7. Enter at 10 and come out at 8.

8. Continue like this to the end of the required section. Finish in the same way as in step 10 on page 81.

Infills

In order to infill in Mazahua-style embroidery, close parallel lines of identical stitches are worked (as described on pages 74–77, 80–81 and 82–83). They can be made thicker and varied with colours. No more than five colours are ever used in a single piece.

An embroidery from the back.

84

The same embroidery from the front.

A finished embroidery from the back.

The same embroidery from the front.

Zigzag

As before, I have numbered the holes in the aida to make it easier to follow the method of working this stitch.

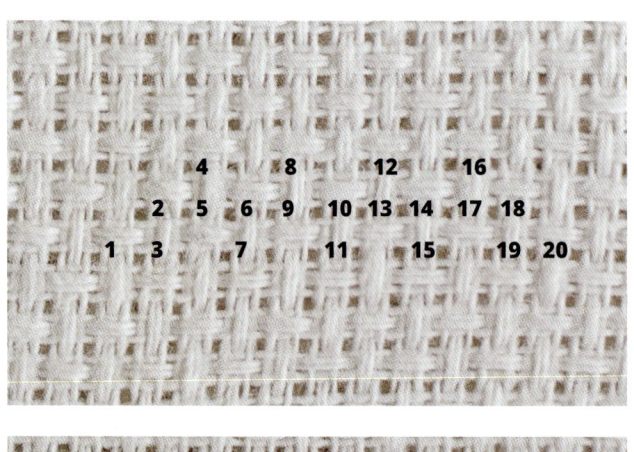

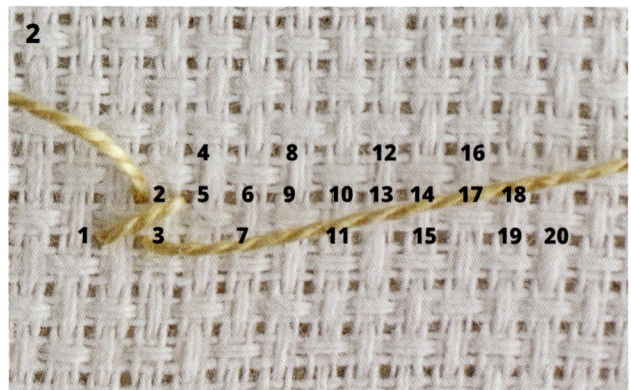
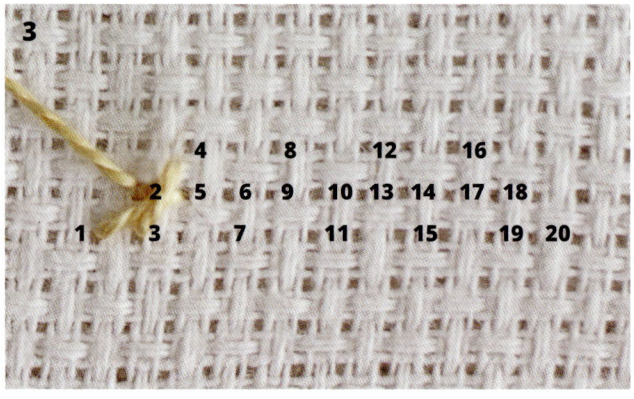

1. Enter at 2 and come out at 1, leaving a short thread tail on the front of the work.

2. Enter at 5 and come out at 3. The tail can be trimmed off at this stage.

3. Enter at 4 and come out at 2.

4. Enter at 6 and come out at 4.

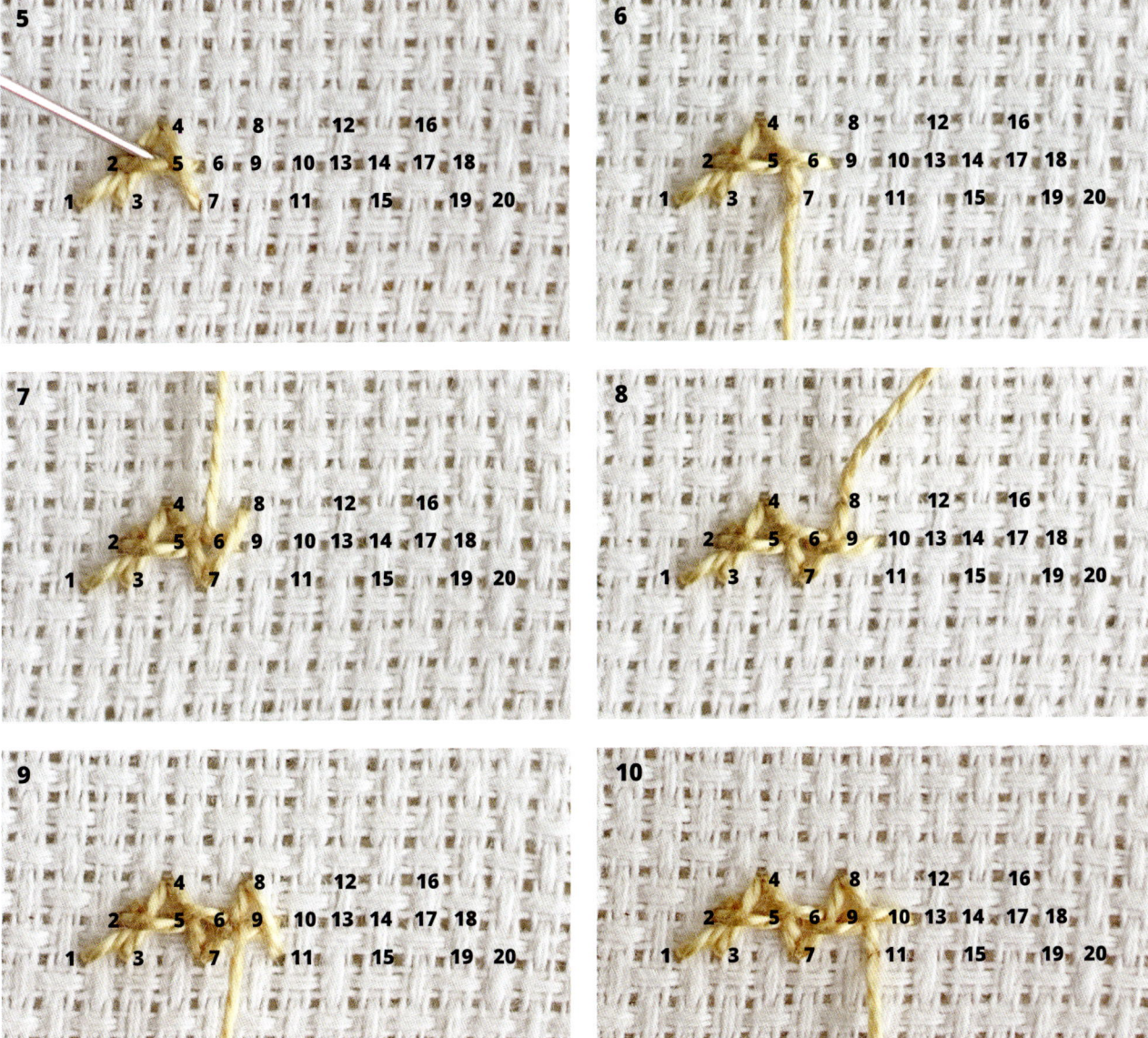

5. Enter at 7 and come out at 5.

6. Enter at 9 and come out at 7.

7. Enter at 8 and come out at 6.

8. Enter at 10 and come out at 8.

9. Enter at 11 and come out at 9.

10. Enter at 13 and come out at 11.

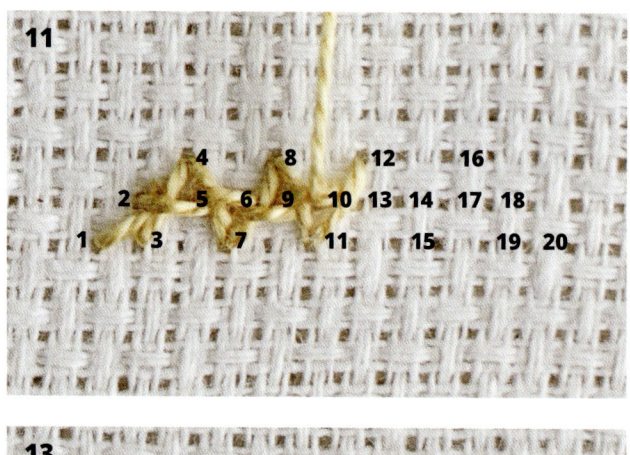

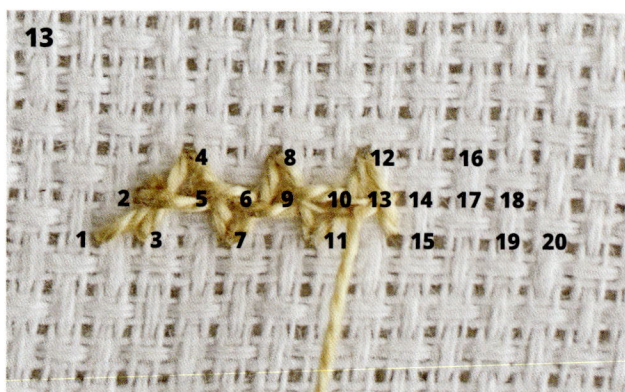
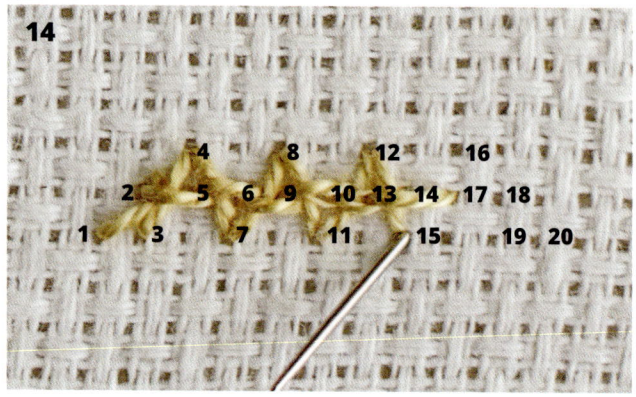
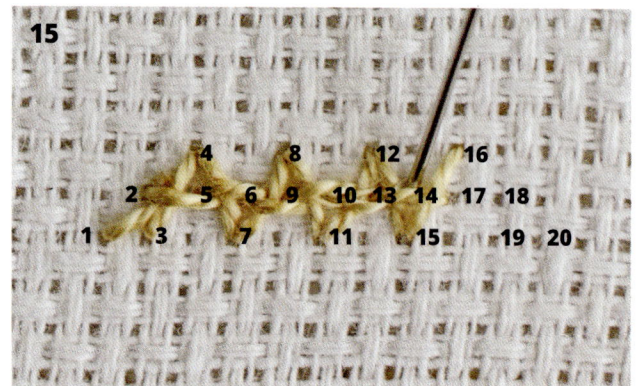

11. Enter at 12 and come out at 10.

12. Enter at 14 and come out at 12.

13. Enter at 15 and come out at 13.

14. Enter at 17 and come out at 15.

15. Enter at 16 and come out at 14.

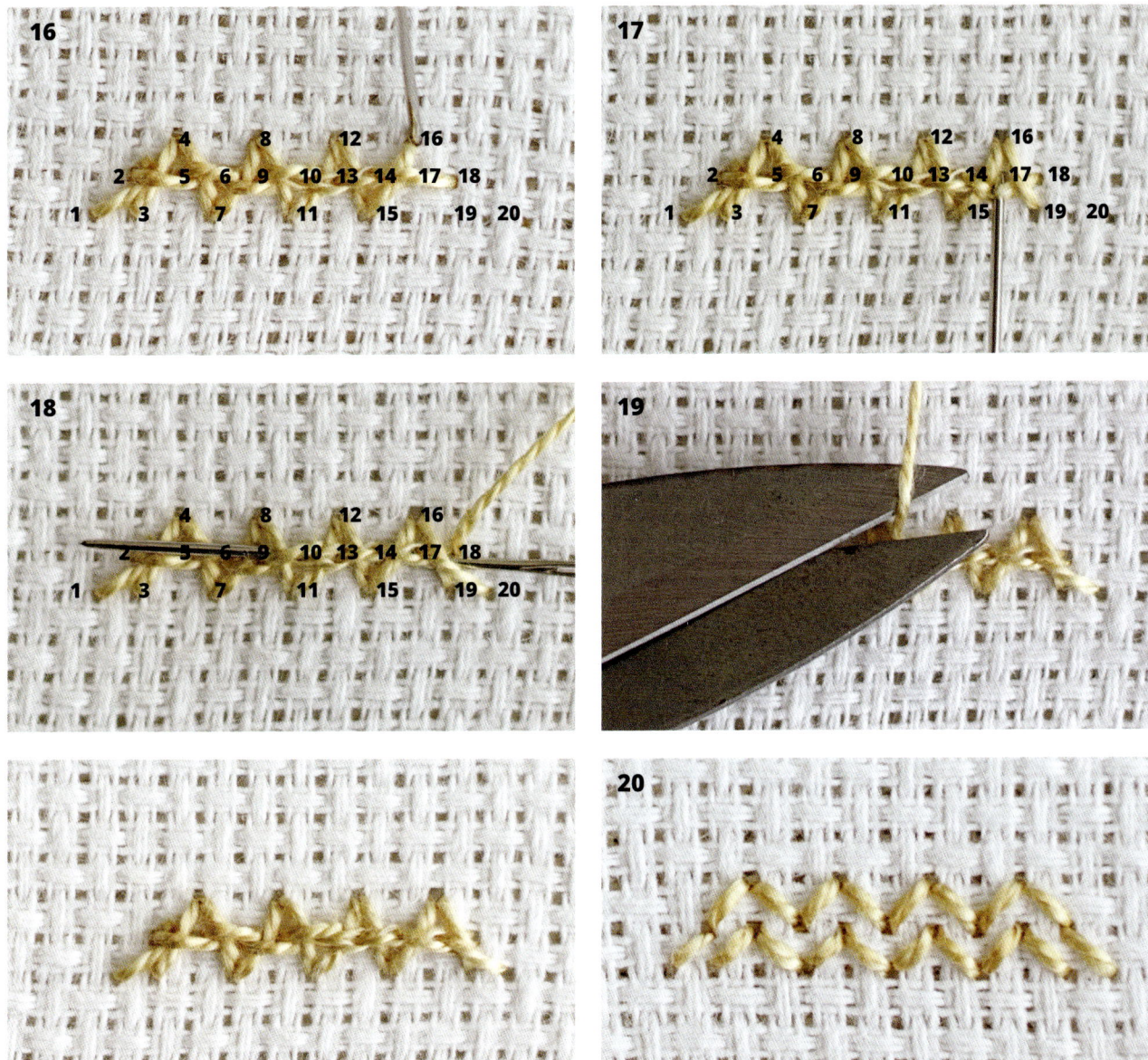

16. Enter at 18 and come out at 16.

17. Enter at 19 and come out at 17.

18. Enter at 20 to remain symmetrical and come out at 18 to finish. To secure the thread, first run it under a few stitches on the front of the work.

19. Finish by cutting off the excess.

20. If the stitch has been worked correctly, on the reverse you will have parallel zigzag lines.

A finished embroidery from the back.

The same embroidery from the front.

Moon

Once again, I have numbered the holes in the aida to make it easier to follow the working method. Note that you may prefer how this stitch looks on the other side of the fabric – see page 97.

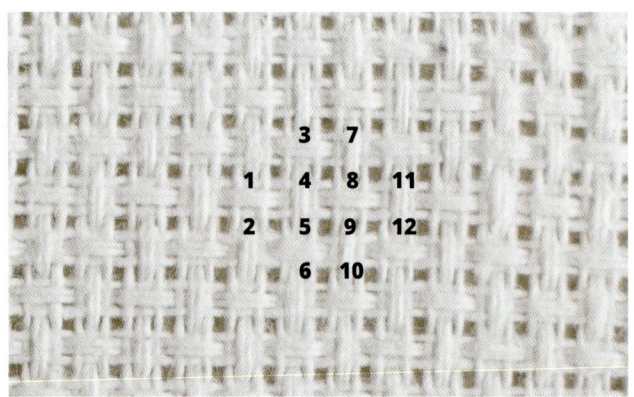

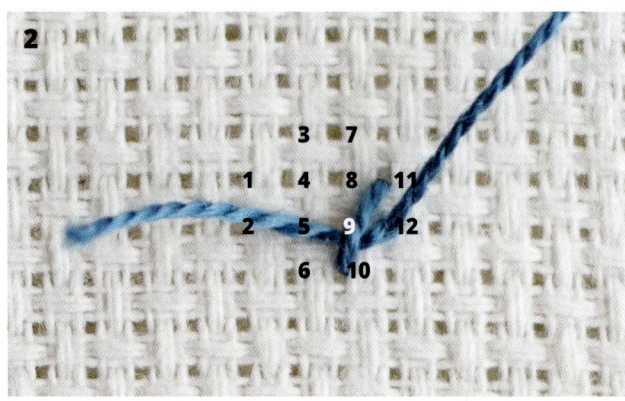
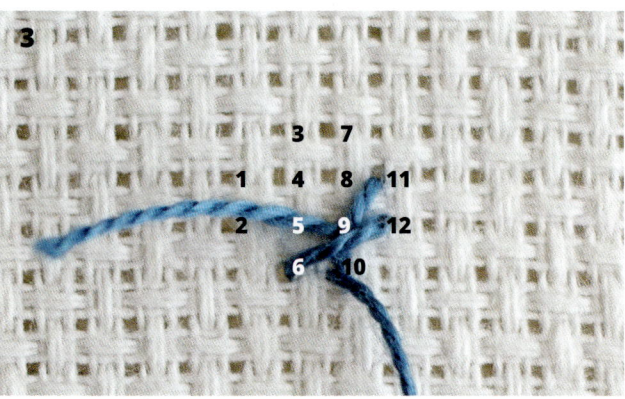
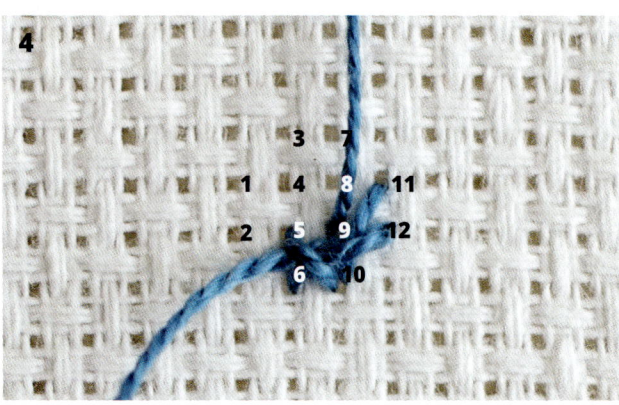

1. Enter at 12 and come out at 11, leaving a short thread tail on the front of the work.

2. Enter at 10 and come out at 12 (leaving the thread tail at the start to be stitched over and hidden).

3. Enter at 6 and come out at 10.

4. Enter at 5 and come out at 9.

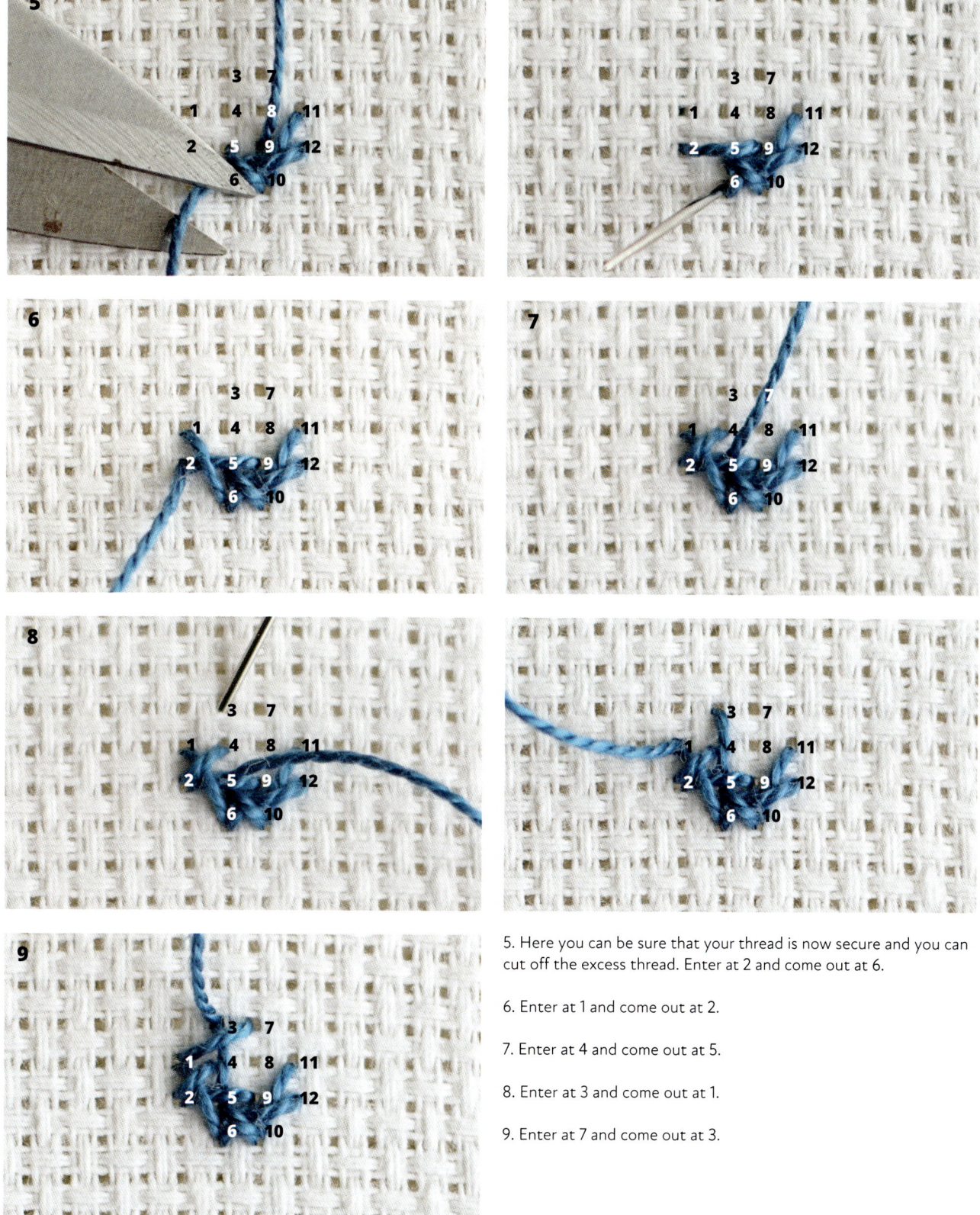

5. Here you can be sure that your thread is now secure and you can cut off the excess thread. Enter at 2 and come out at 6.

6. Enter at 1 and come out at 2.

7. Enter at 4 and come out at 5.

8. Enter at 3 and come out at 1.

9. Enter at 7 and come out at 3.

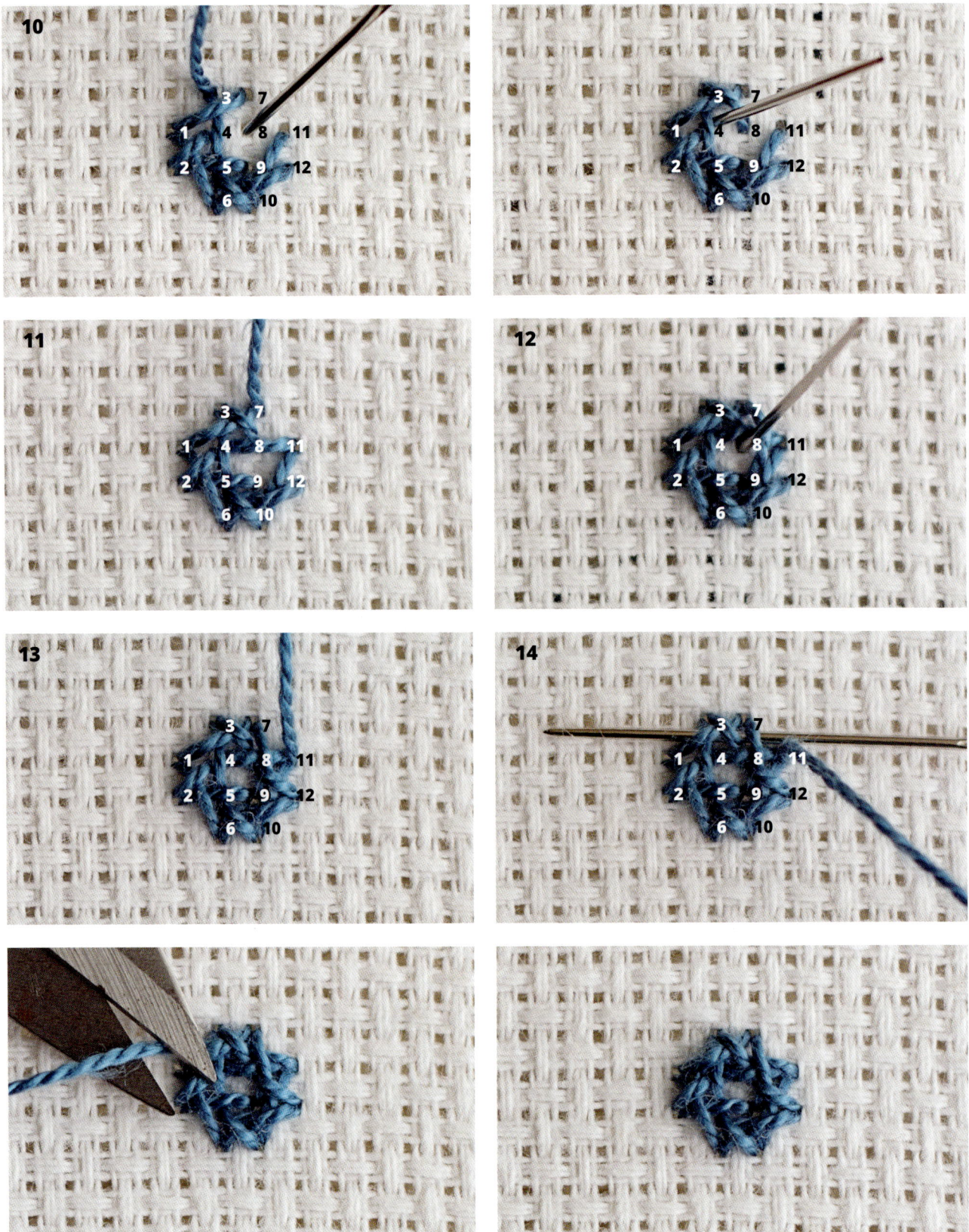

A well-worked moon should have an outline like this on the reverse side. Sometimes this stitch is used in reverse as the back of the work is also highly decorative.

10. Enter at 8 and come out at 4.

11. Enter at 11 and come out at 7.

12. Enter at 9 and come out at 8.

13. Enter at 12 and come out at 11.

14. Weave the needle under the threads (between 7 and 8) at the top of the motif to secure the thread and then trim off the tail.

Eye

Note that this stitch is worked from the back of the fabric, although if you want a solid eye you could work it from the front. As before, I have numbered the holes in the aida to make it easier to follow the working method.

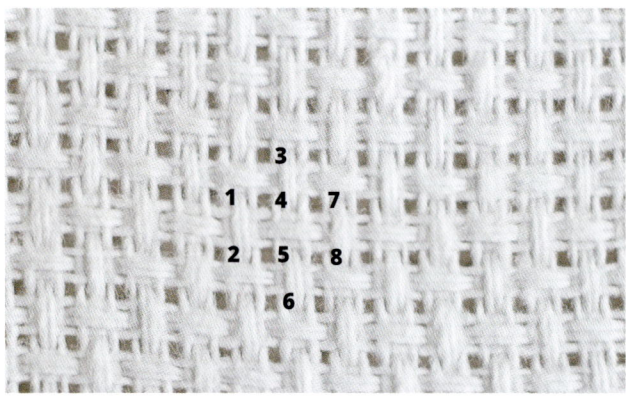

1. Working with the wrong side of the fabric facing you for the result shown on page 103, enter at 4 and come out at 5, leaving a short thread tail.

2. Enter at 7 and come out at 8.

3. Go back in at 4 and come out at 5.

4. Cut off the tail of thread.

5. Enter at 3 and come out at 7.

6. Enter at 1 and come out at 3.

7. Enter at 2 and come out at 1.

8. Enter at 6 and come out at 2.

9. Enter at 8 and come out at 6.

10. Slide the needle upwards under the stitches, pull through and trim off the thread end.

The finished stitch from the front.

With this stitch, the eye is revealed when you turn the fabric over.

Interlinked hearts

This all might look complicated – but don't panic. The rhythm of Mazahua embroidery is very logical, almost mathematical, and the brain absorbs this sequence based on repetition. I have numbered the holes in the aida to make it easier to follow the working method.

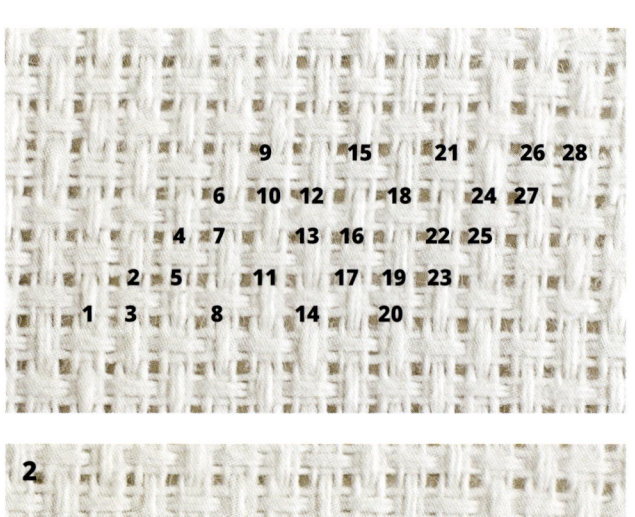

1. Enter at 2 and come out at 1, leaving a short thread tail on the front of the work.

2. Enter at 5 and come out at 3.

3. Enter at 4 and come out at 2. Cut away the tail of thread.

4. Enter at 7 and come out at 5.

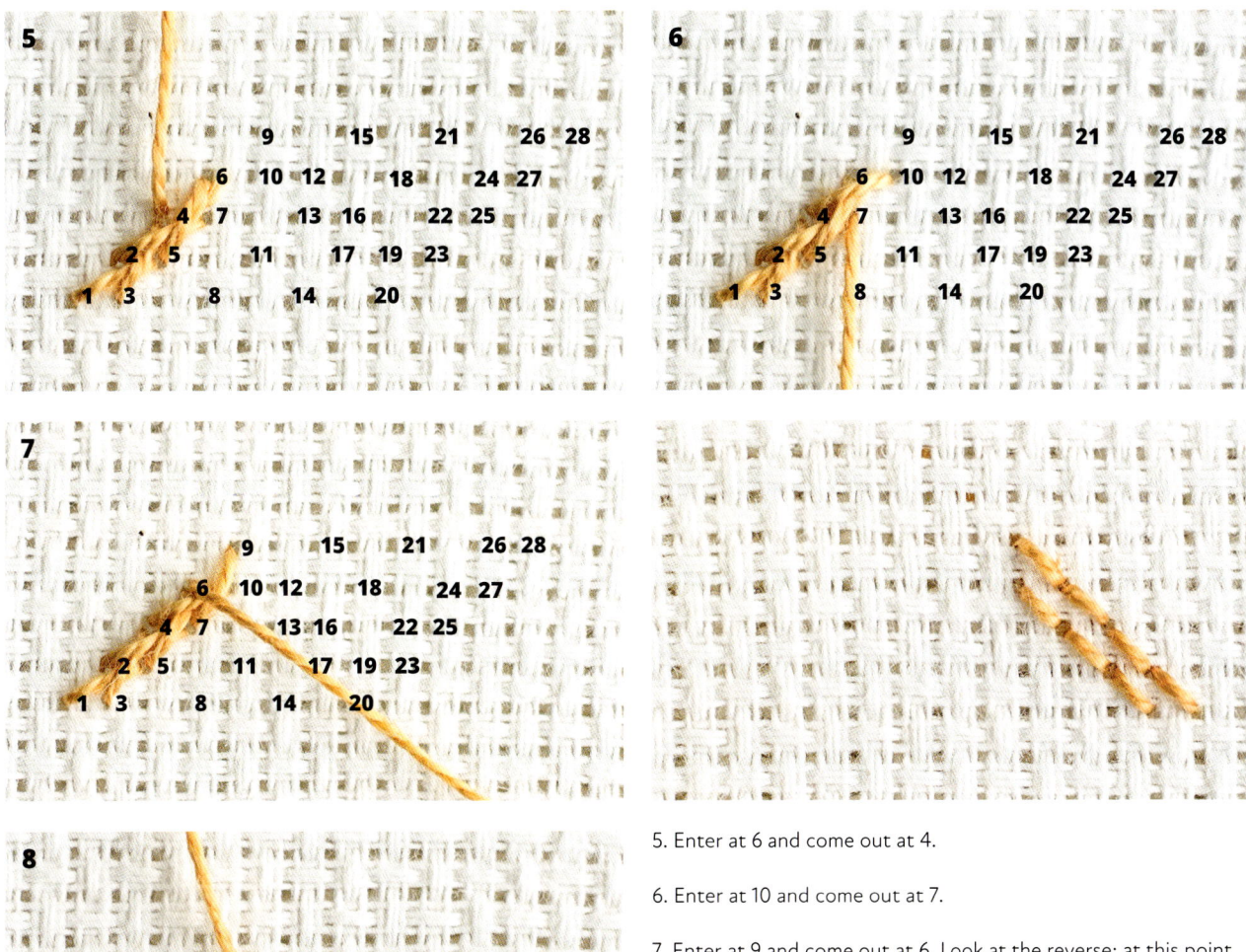

5. Enter at 6 and come out at 4.

6. Enter at 10 and come out at 7.

7. Enter at 9 and come out at 6. Look at the reverse; at this point you should have a diagonal of four stitches on the long line and three stitches on the shorter line. If that is so, you can continue. If there are too few, continue to work until you have the correct number of stitches. If there are too many, go back and undo the excess stitches.

8. Enter at 12 and come out at 9.

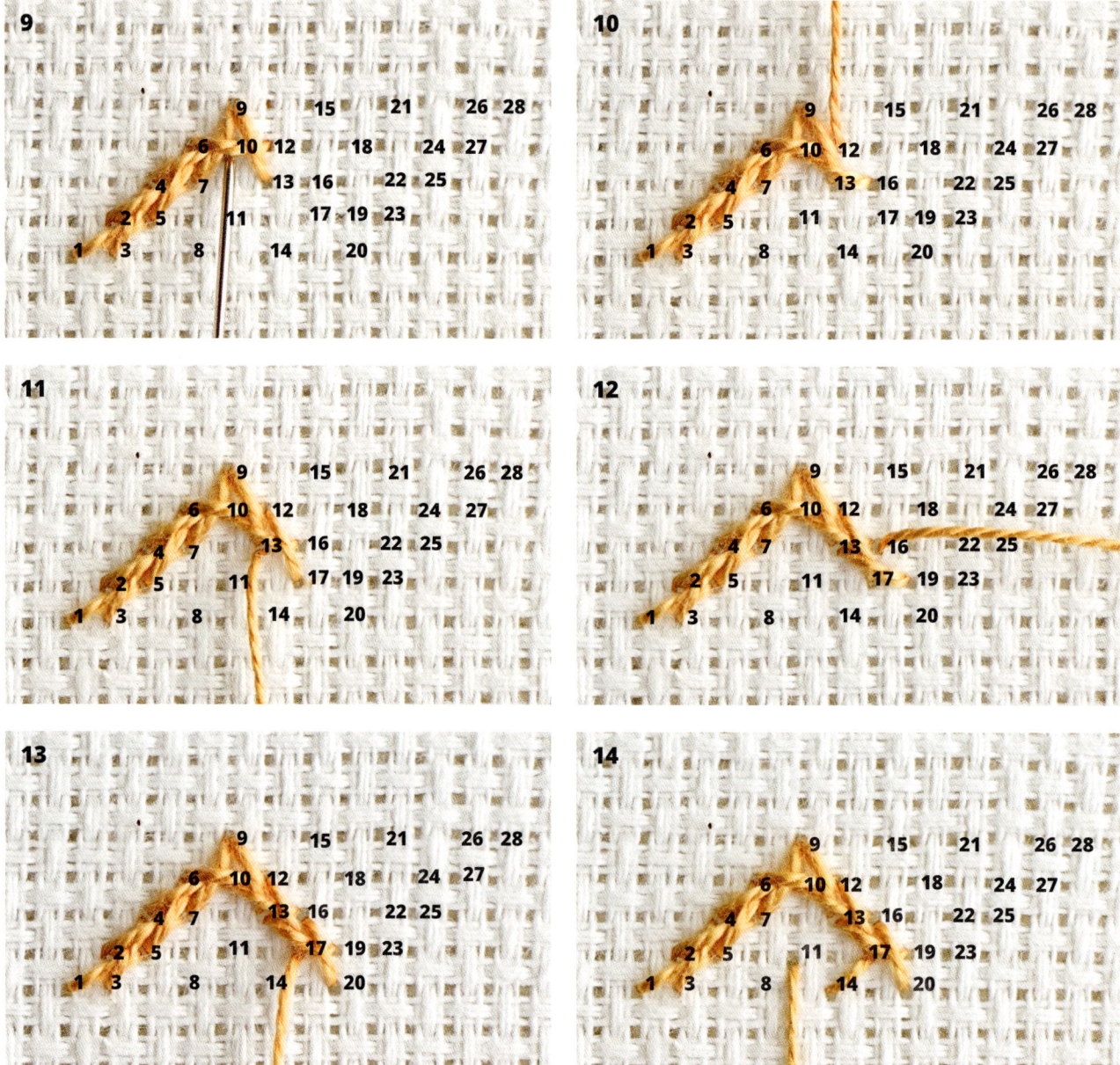

9. Enter at 13 and come out at 10.

10. Enter at 16 and come out at 12.

11. Enter at 17 and come out at 13.

12. Enter at 19 and come out at 16.

13. Enter at 20 and come out at 17.

14. Enter at 14 and come out at 11.

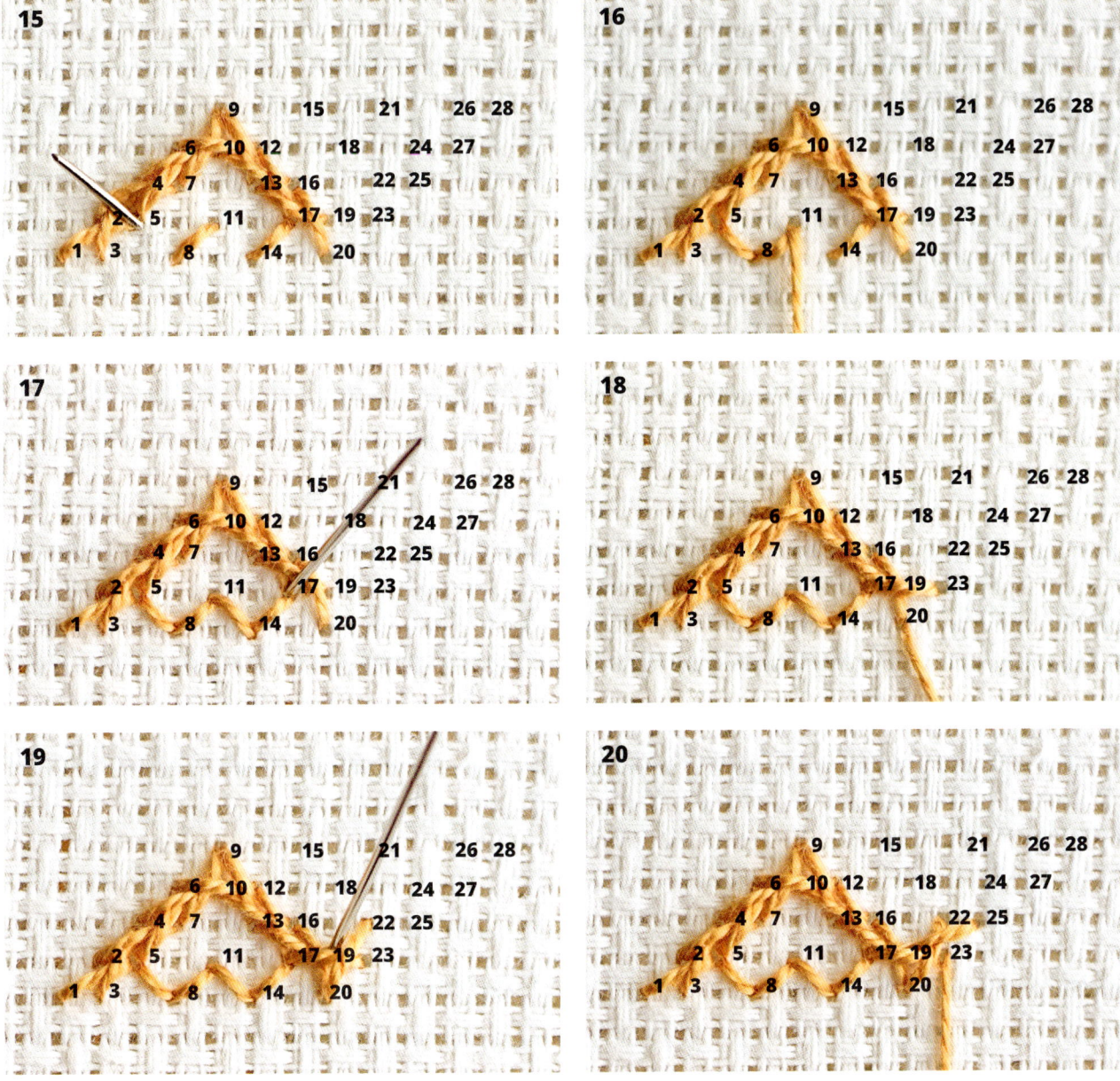

15. Enter at 8 and come out at 5.

16. Enter at 8 and come out at 11.

17. Enter at 14 and come out at 17. At this point the first, inverted, heart has been formed.

18. Enter at 23 and come out at 20.

19. Enter at 22 and come out at 19.

20. Enter at 25 and come out at 23.

21. Enter at 24 and come out at 22.

22. Enter at 27 and come out at 25.

23. Enter at 26 and come out at 24.

24. Enter at 21 and come out at 18.

25. Enter at 15 and come out at 12.

26. Enter at 15 and come out at 18.

27. Enter at 21 and come out at 24. The second heart is complete.

28. Enter at 28 to complete the design.

You can continue the heart pattern and make it as long as you wish. (You can see this stitch on the piece shown on pages 86–87.)

A finished embroidery from the back.

The same embroidery from the front.

Toninero embroidery

San Antonino Castillo Velasco, Oaxaca

In the state of Oaxaca, San Antonino is a happy, verdant town that smells of citrus. It was not easy, however, to track down the famous embroidery of birds and flowers.

Upon arriving in the town, we asked around for someone who could inform us about the typical embroidery of the region. In one shop we met an elderly lady called Juana Aguilar, who told us that another lady, who had dedicated herself to embroidery, had a stall near the market and that her name was Severa Santiago. She had also told us that the thread used was red wool, and very heavy.

Juana Aguilar told us, regretfully, that she had sold her own traditional costume, and she also explained that very few people now wear it or have the original.

It was not difficult to recognize Mrs Santiago amongst the other embroiderers who gather in the market. She was a very old lady but was sitting without slouching. There was something in her that I recognized: a very specific dignity of someone dedicated to embroidery, a task that brings us into harmony regardless of origin and age. I brought out my drawings; I had been drawing the motifs of San Antonino since I fell in love with its embroidery after having seen some samples in the Museum of Decorative Arts in Mexico City, and I gave her one.

Mrs Santiago told us how she had also sold her traditional costume in order to buy medicine. But she makes her own clothes and also made them for her grandchildren when they were little; now they no longer want them.

Here the women inherit the position of embroiderer. In each of their pieces they show the landscape of flowers in which, according to their ancestors, the Heroic Town of San Antonino was built. The language spoken in the area is *Zapoteco* or *Diidxazá*. The production of one of these pieces may take up to six months.

Mrs Santiago's story worries me, especially living in the social and political environment of Oaxaca. In political adverts the women are dressed in the typical costume using it as a town flag, but nobody uses it in the streets. They are using the combination of wool and cotton of San Antonino as an identifying link to the community. Those in political power, through their propaganda, appropriate an image, recognized by all inhabitants, to gain their trust through the lost costume. No inhabitants of the city currently wear it, and there are also very few people who even keep the familiar costume – only those who dance in *Los Lunes de Cerro*[1] or the fiestas.

Embroidery in the community is so important that they dress the images of the *Virgen de Juquila* and the *Virgen del Carmen* with delicate pieces worked over months as a gift to the town's patron saints.

For this type of work, known colloquially as Toninero embroidery, satin mouliné thread is used to embroider the pansies that dominate the design. This thread is much more difficult to use than cotton, as it tangles very easily, although the brilliance of the thread gives it an exceptional finish.

Toninero embroidery is very laborious, and the embroidery thread is difficult to work. The technique in this work is, therefore, very important.

---

[1] 'Mondays on the Hill', an annual cultural event that takes place on the last two Mondays in July, in Oaxaca.

There is no name for the stitch that is used to work Toninero embroidery as there is only the one. It is an interesting stitch as it is the one that is closest to drawing.

We are going to work with a large-eyed no. 26 embroidery needle, 2/4 in satin thread (two threads, doubled in the needle so you are working with four).

There are two types of flower: the detailed ones and the plain ones. The interlinking of both is what gives movement to the image.

For the petals of the detailed flowers, choose two colours. Among these you will include black and yellow, which are the base colours for this motif.

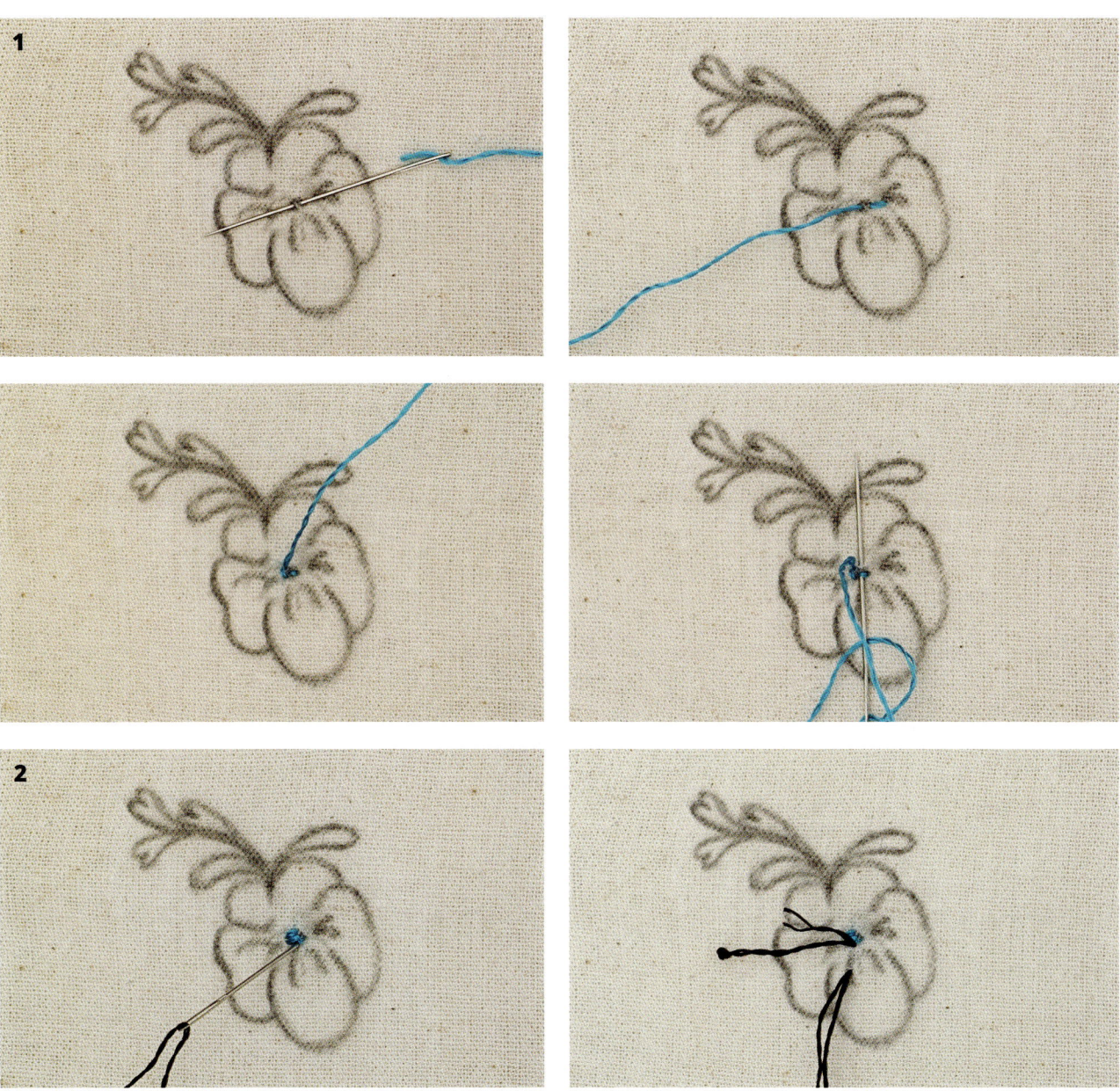

1. In Toninero embroidery no knots are made, so start by taking a tiny stitch in the centre with one of the colours for the petals, leaving a 2–3mm (⅛in) tail on the right side of the fabric. Go in again and out at the same point in order to secure the thread and cover the tail, then do another couple of small stitches in the centre.

2. Change to black thread, secure the thread in the same way and embroider around the centre with straight stitches of different lengths in a starburst formation. Don't forget to trim off the excess thread once you have secured it, to avoid it getting tangled. Remember that this thread is delicate.

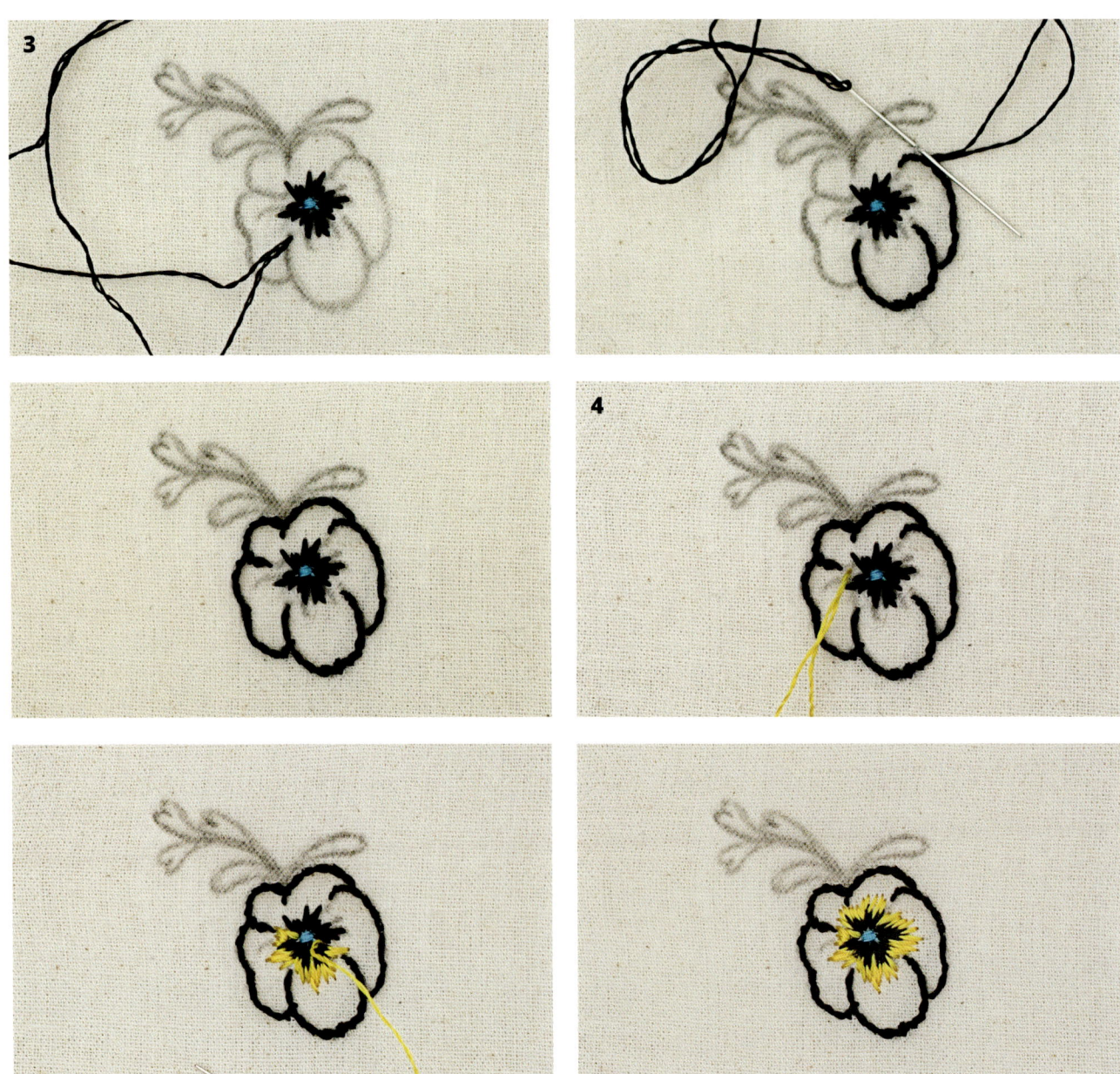

3. With the same black thread, outline the petals of the flower with backstitch (called stem stitch in the UK/US – see pages 28–29).

4. Change to yellow thread and work more straight stitches around the flower centre, starting to direct the stitches towards the petals.

5

5. Change to one of the colours that you chose for the petals (dark blue, here); secure as before and continue stitching from the centre outwards within one petal. The stitch is simple – it is basic infilling. Pass the needle in and out of the fabric – you just have to give direction and volume to the form with the direction of the stitches.

6. Repeat with the petal opposite.

6

7. Continue to infill the alternate petals with the colour you chose for the flower centre.

8. Finish on the reverse by weaving the needle through some of the threads on the back and trim off the excess.

9. Play with shades of green with the same stitch and process to add stalks and leaves.

To embroider the plain flowers, the same stitch is used but in a single colour and with no outline.

A finished embroidery from the back.

The same embroidery from the front.

Mixe embroidery

Oaxaca de Juárez, Oaxaca

Adelita was an Oaxaca Mixe[1] who helped my mother with the household chores from when I was 10 years old. She was an affectionate, smiley lady and in addition to looking after the house, she looked after my brother and me. She became part of the family. My parents are godparents to her children, and I remember that I hated the long journey to the fiestas in her town when I was a child. All of the Mixe words that I know she taught me and I miss her a lot.

Ayuujk and Mixe are synonymous. The territorial space of the Ayuujk is drawn by bilingual indigenous people, whose maternal language is *Ayuujk*. Their territorial settlement is defined by an ecological niche in the highland area of the Mixe district, on the sides of the mountains of Cempoaltépetl, located in the northern sierra of the state of Oaxaca. Cempoaltépetl is the centre of the universe and a sacred hill in the origin stories of these people and their community.

In addition to the relevance that Mixe embroidery has taken on in the last few years, for me it was important to include it in this book. Like the odd Mixe words that came back to my memory while I was working on this chapter, the embroidery also returned. Although originally done by machine, the translation to hand stitch was important not only to me but also for the 'awesome' embroiderers – strong, serious, feisty women, according to Edith, one of Adelita's daughters – of the Oaxaca sierra. They told me that a long time ago it was also done by hand, but I think these were just comments to liven up the chat, as I have never seen an Ayuujk piece made by hand that is more than five years old.

After embroidering by hand one has a better understanding of one's project, the embroidery is conceived in another way and even appears to be something else. Like Adelita, who in reality was called Obdulia, but we called her Adela because her children could never pronounce her name.

Mixe embroidery is in reality very simple, but it is precisely this simplicity that turns it into a very elegant type of embroidery. Only two colours are used: black and red, the shade of the latter depending on the embroiderer but usually tending towards wine and purple. There is a very rigid symbolism in the community in relation to colour and, unlike other communities, the embroiderers work alone in their homes.

So that the line remains fine, a sewing thread is used instead of embroidery thread, with a long, flexible needle with a medium-sized eye for sewing (like a milliner's or straw needle). There is no better way of understanding the importance and plasticity of the needle than through embroidery.

In this type of work a single stitch is used, with which all designs are created, called *mujxp*, which in Mixe means 'that which germinates'. This stitch is a 'line' stitch very much like Holbein stitch, which is used for Assisi work.

---

[1] Indigenous person of Oaxaca.

STITCHES
Mixe

This is a medium-sized straight stitch worked along the lines of the design. In Mixe embroidery no knots are made, so start from the front of the work.

This stitch has been worked with a single sewing thread, on a size 16 chenille needle, on cotton fabric.

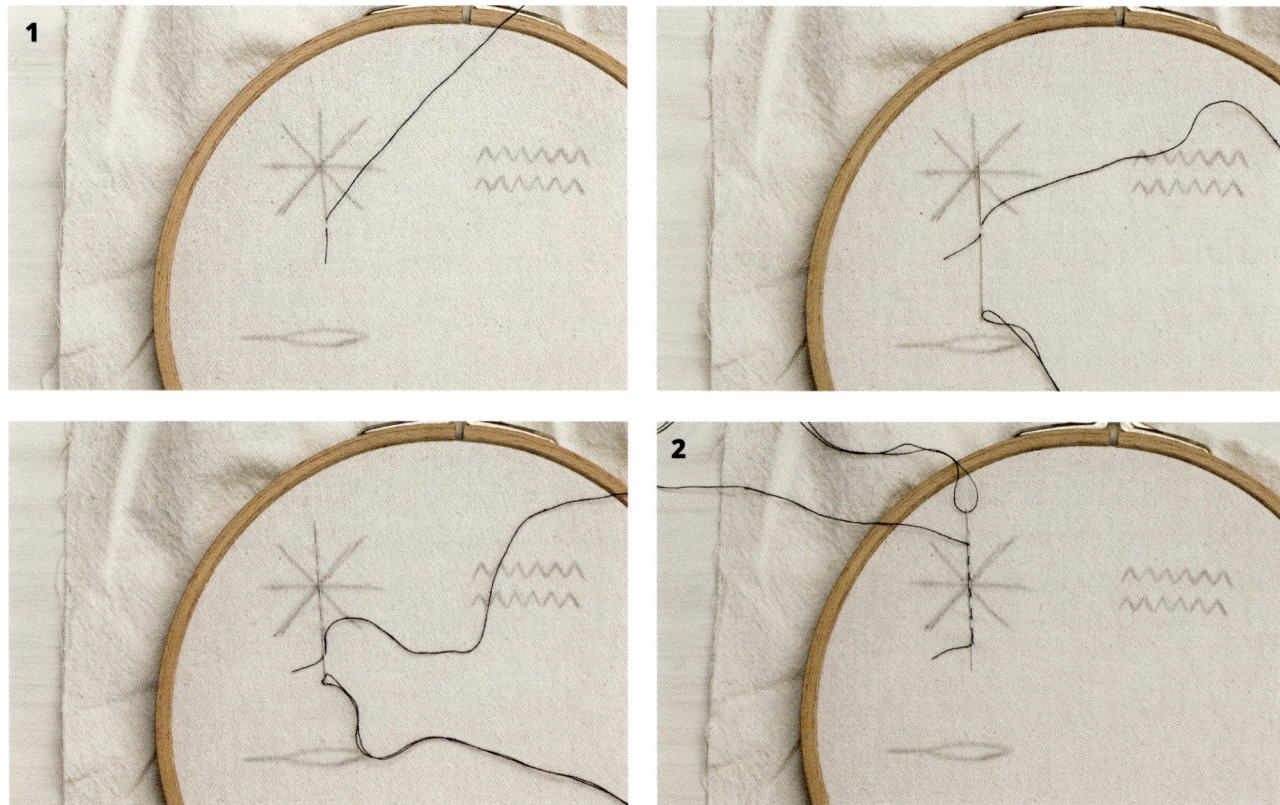

1. Take a small stitch, leaving a short thread tail on the right side of the fabric. Go through the same stitch again to secure the thread.

2. Work small running stitches along the design line, ensuring that the spaces that you leave are uniform.

3. Return on the same line, filling in the gaps with your stitches to create a solid line.

4. Cut off the thread tail at the start of the embroidery and continue working the stitches until the motif is complete.

5. To finish, weave through the threads on the reverse and trim off the excess.

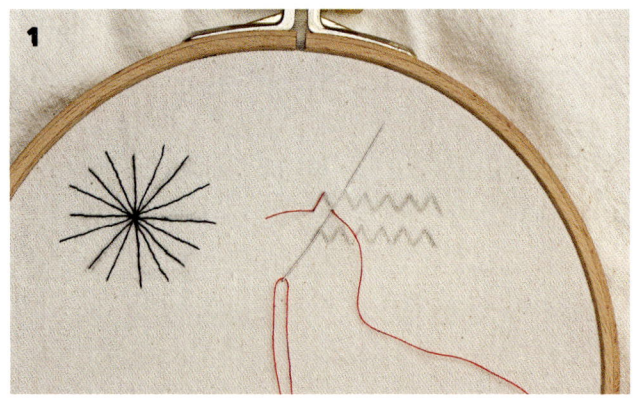

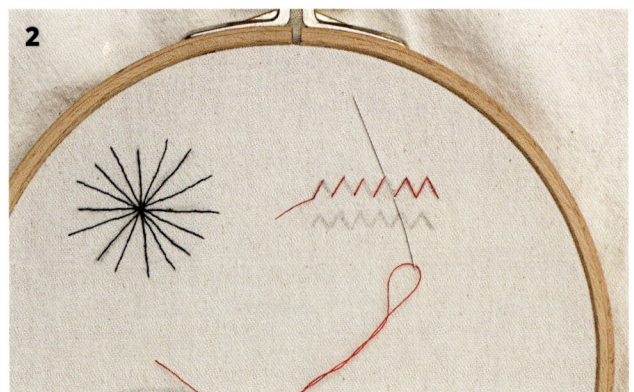

To create zigzag lines, you work one side first (all the upward-facing stitches), then return to the other (downward-facing stitches).

1. Starting with no knot, first do all the lines leaning in one direction.

2. Return, embroidering the opposite lines.

3. Finish on the reverse (see page 24), then cut away the starting thread tail.

1. Infilling within the embroidery is also done with straight stitches, one line next to another.

2. The colours are embroidered one over the other.

A finished embroidery from the back.

The same embroidery from the front.

Purépecha embroidery

Tzintzuntzan, Michoacán

I remember the road to Michoacán. Arriving in Tzintzuntzan after so much anticipation, everything seemed a little smaller and more incredible. I remember the people from the lake, families of three people who live on an income of between 50 and 300 pesos[1] depending on 'how well the fishing goes'. Net fishing is important in Tzintzuntzan and although I searched for similarities with embroidery, there was not much to be found. Fishing is a man's thing while the sale of fish and embroidery are women's things.

We spent a lot of time travelling by road, the landscape surrounded by hills, more like small mountains, but they were mountains covered with flowers not trees, as if the trees stayed small or the flowers in Michoacán were large. The crows seem like black bastions amongst the white clouds, thousands of them pecking here and there, with a mischievous 'cruac', which sounded like stealing to me.

Tzintzuntzan, whose name means 'place of hummingbirds', was one of the most important Purépecha capitals during the pre-Hispanic period. It resisted various attempts at conquest on the part of the Aztec empire, which gave it the title of a feudal estate, and it reached 40,000 inhabitants. Today it is home to flowers, fish and a type of embroidery that could not be more beautiful.

I did not stay in Tzintzuntzan – I stayed in Ichupio, a town that is very close by, where my host, Veva, lived with her husband Iván and her daughter Guadalupe, two years and eight months old, as she herself repeatedly pointed out every time the occasion arose.

We were sleeping in a *toje*, a very large cabin with a bread oven in the basement. When it was cold they made bread and the heat rose to warm the house. In the same way as there were crows on the road during the day, at night, there were clouds of bats. And by the third night I had managed to get used to the screeching.

Very early, when Mr Iván returned with the fish, we went with Veva down to Tzintzuntzan so that she could sell the fish while I learned to embroider. A stitch here, a stitch there; smiles. Pedro bought us coffee and I gave the vendor embroiderers' perlé thread; they liked it a lot and began to include it in their work.

The language spoken in the region is *Purépecha* and it has very specific characteristics that classify it as an isolated language, as it has no common etymology with any other language spoken today or previously in Mexico. It is said that Purépecha sounds like the song of a turtle dove and, like most of the country's languages, it is in the process of disappearing.

In Purépecha embroidery the knots on the reverse are not important. You can make a discreet knot to hold the stitch and nothing happens. It is something that I like; I think of it as a turtle dove knot because in Tzintzuntzan, where the people sound like turtle doves, knots are good.

Pínandini and *pínasku* are infill stitches. *Misiri, uni* and *juramuti* are ornamental stitches. To show these stitches I will use 3/6 mouliné thread (three threads used double in the needle), a needle with a point and a blunt (tapestry) needle. In Michoacán they liked the perlé thread that I shared so much that there is no doubt that, within a short time, the thread used in the pieces will be that.

Purépecha infill stitches work rather well as they are easy stitches to do and serve to cover an area quickly.

[1] Equating to roughly GBP £2–£12 / US $0.27–$16 / CAN $0.38–$23 at the time of going to print.

STITCHES
Pínandini
(silence)

The stitches in this chapter have been worked over canvas using a size 3 mouliné thread used double (although you can use it single if you prefer), with both a no. 24 Sharps needle and blunt needle.

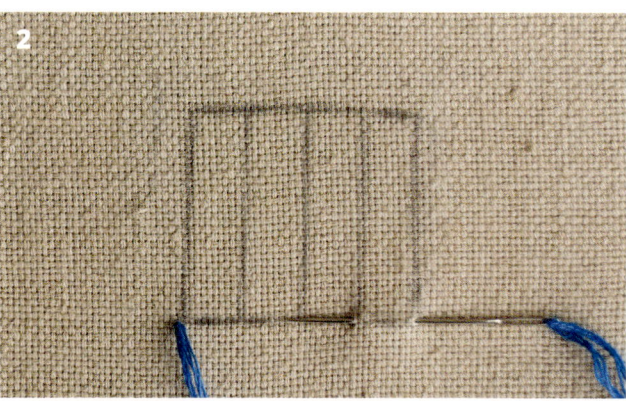
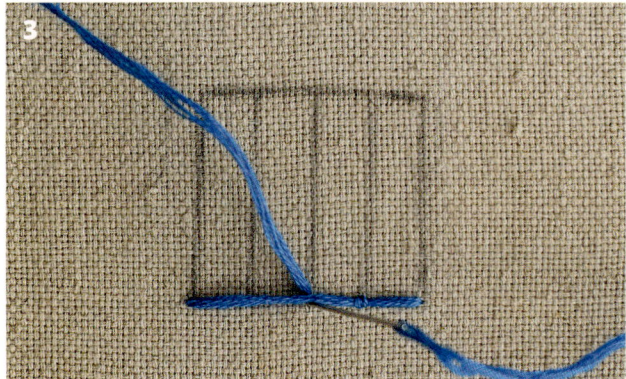
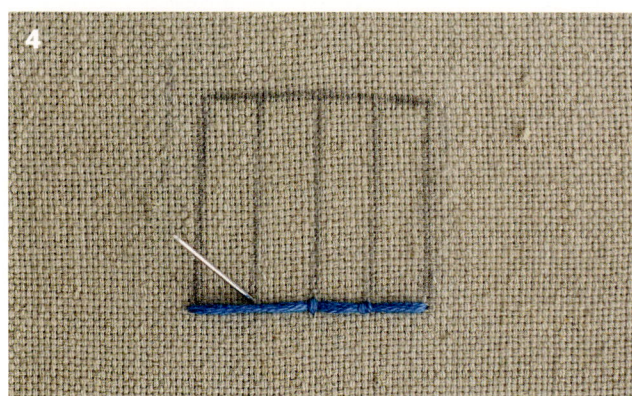

1. For this infill stitch I will divide the area to be covered into columns that will mark the positions of the couching stitches.

2. With a sharp needle, bring the thread out on the bottom left of the shape, go in at the bottom right and come out at the first line that marks the couching positions.

3. Take a small stitch (couching stitch) over the long thread to secure it and bring the needle out at the next marked line. Repeat to the last marked line.

4. Take a couching stitch over the thread on the final line and then bring the needle out on the left-hand side, just above the first long stitch, ready to repeat the process. The couching stitches secure the long stitches and add texture.

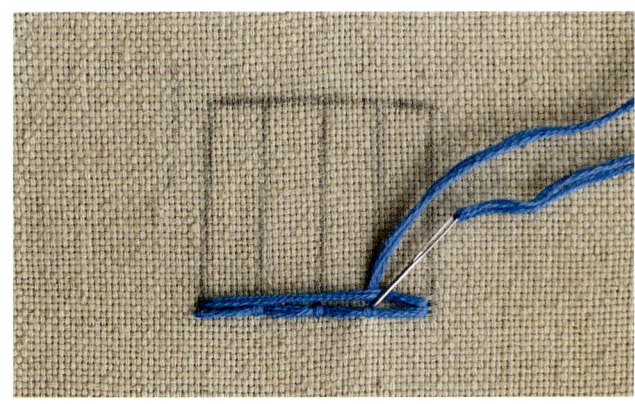
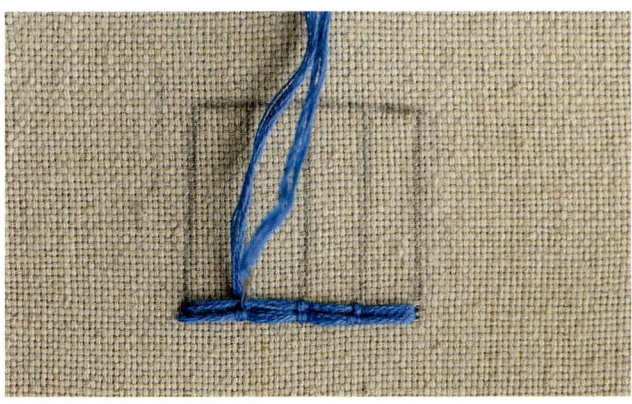
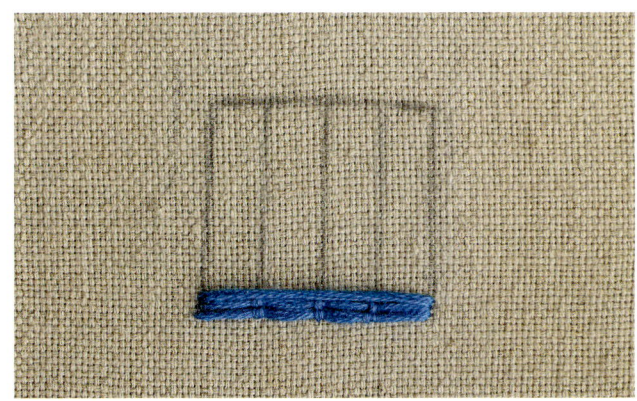

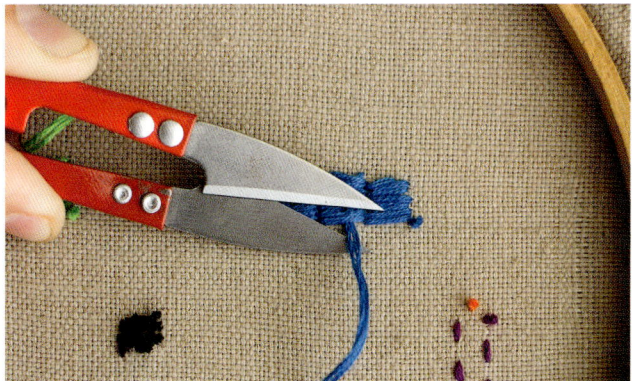

5. Make another long stitch next to the first one and return, securing it in place with couching stitches.

6. Continue in this way to fill the shape.

7. Finish by weaving in the thread on the reverse and cut off the excess.

A finished embroidery from the back.

The same embroidery from the front.

Pínasku
(silence)

This stitch is very similar to *pínandini*: it is more of a variant. In fact, *pínandini* and *pínasku* are two different words for referring to silence.

Unlike *pínandini*, this time the columns are on the diagonal. The stitch is worked and used in more or less the same way.

1. Mark the positions of the couching stitches with diagonal lines.

2. With a sharp needle, bring the thread out on the bottom left of the shape, go in at the bottom right and come out at the first diagonal line.

3. Take a small stitch (couching stitch) over the long thread to secure it and bring the needle out at the next marked line. Repeat to the last marked line.

4. Take a couching stitch over the thread on the final line and then bring the needle out on the left-hand side, just above the first long stitch, ready to repeat the process. The couching stitches secure the long stitches and add texture.

5. Make another long stitch next to the first one and return, fixing it in place with couching stitches.

6. These couching stitches create a secondary pattern over the filling.

7. Continue in this way to fill the shape.

A finished embroidery from the back.

The same embroidery from the front.

Misiri
(sparks of fire)

This stitch is very good to use for petals, leaves and even on its own, as it is very simple and elegant. You may know it as detached chain stitch or lazy daisy stitch.

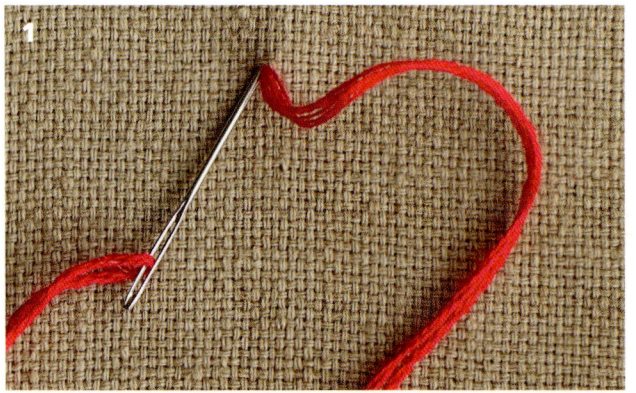

1. Using a sharp needle, bring your thread out where you want the stitch to be, then take it back down in the same place without pulling all the thread through.

2. Bring the needle back out where you want the other end of the *misiri* to be and then pull on the thread until the loop of the stitch is the desired size.

3. Pull the needle out and take a short (couching) stitch over the end of the loop to secure it.

4. Do not put too much pressure on the stitch as it may lose the shape of a teardrop. You can adjust the position of the thread with the eye of the needle.

Uni
(bone)

There is a family of stitches that is not worked into the fabric itself, but is worked on a base of other stitches called 'foundation stitches'. A foundation, which varies from stitch to stitch, is embroidered first, and then the decorative stitch is worked over this. This particular stitch – *uni* – is also known as raised chain band stitch.

1. For *uni*, the foundation is a line of simple parallel straight stitches made using a sharp needle. Make these as short or long as you wish.

2. Change to a blunt (tapestry) needle. I will change colour to make the images clearer, but if you wish not to see the foundation stitch, it is better to use the same colour. Bring the needle up just above the top bar and centred. Take the needle over the stitch and back up under it.

3. Pull the thread through.

4. Always keep the working thread below the stitches being worked.

5. Pick up the same foundation stitch, this time from the top, and close the stitch slowly, making sure that the needle goes over the top of the thread.

6. You will see how the working thread closes, giving it the form of a knot or chain that forms the stitch on each foundation stitch.

7. Go to the next foundation stitch and thread the needle up and under it to start the stitch again.

8. Continue in this way to the end.

9. When finished, go through the fabric 3mm (⅛in) from the last stitch and secure the thread on the back. **Note:** at no time is the fabric pierced with the tapestry needle, except in the first and last stitches.

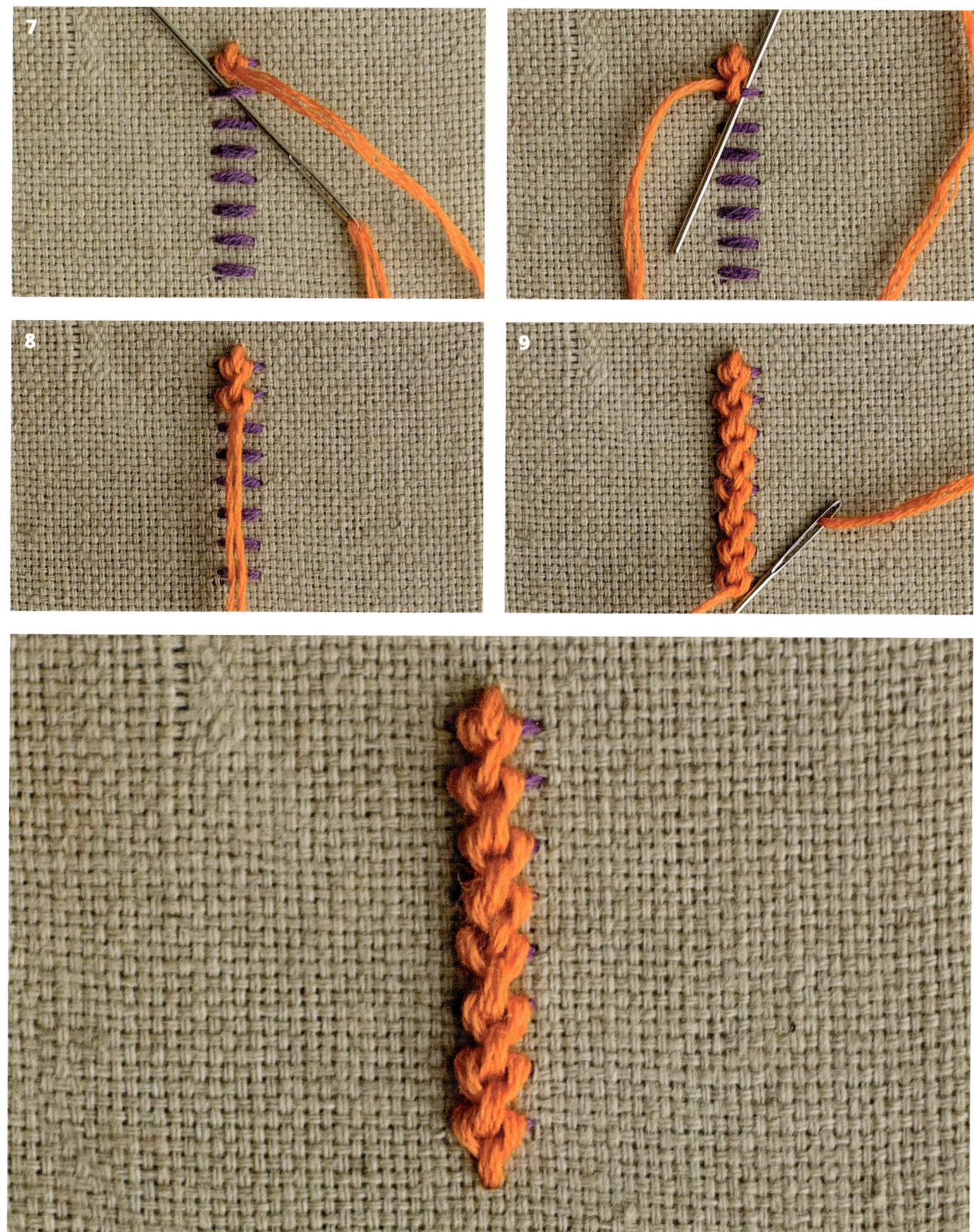

A finished embroidery from the back.

The same embroidery from the front.

Juramuti
(chief)

This stitch creates a beautiful three-dimensional effect, used mainly for figures in Purépecha embroidery.

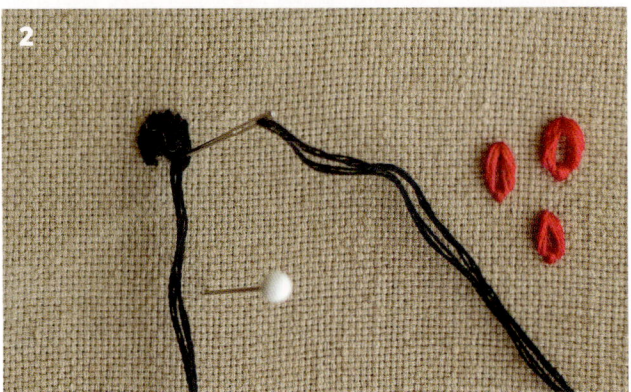

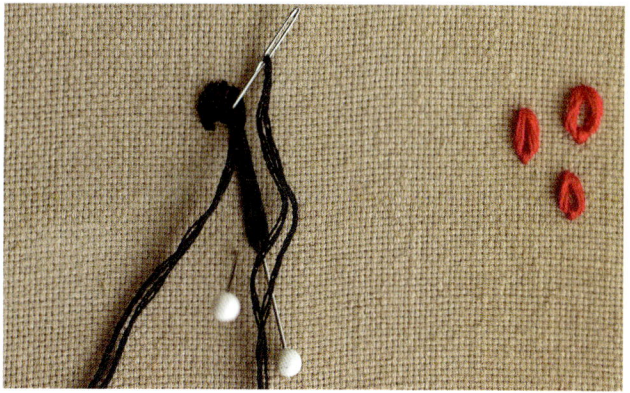

1. Make the head section with normal infilling (satin stitch).

2. At the base of the head, as if you were doing more infill stitches, make long stitch loops without piercing the fabric at the bottom, or putting pressure on the stitch.

3. You can make it easier for yourself by using pins to hold the loops in place.

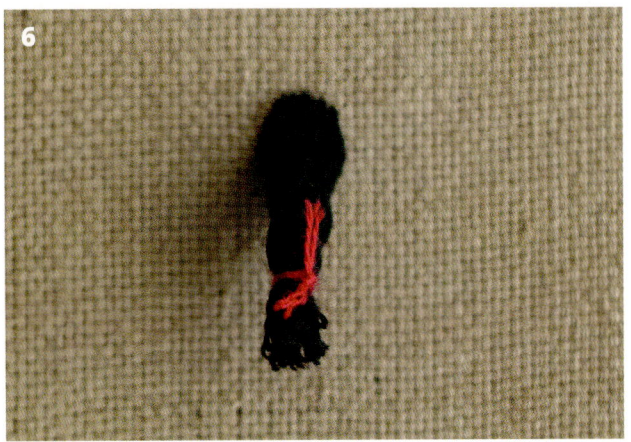

4. Make several stitches like this, which will form the hair. Once complete, weave in and finish on the reverse with care.

5. Remove the pins and cut the loops to open them up into two pieces. Comb a bit with a needle to make the strands more hair-like.

6. Divide the stitches into three thicker strands to make a normal three-strand braid. Finally, secure with a thread of the same colour or choose a contrasting colour.

The braid will lift itself from the fabric, like a floating stitch.

Lavín embroidery

Mexico City

'Embroidery, good embroidery, is and should be considered as a work of art.'

These are the words of the artist and restorer Trinidad Morcillo Raya, born in Granada in 1891. She was one of the first textile artists as we know them now, and a master of the work and lace workshop of the *Escuela de Arte y Oficios Artísticos de Granada*. Her work was not called embroidery but 'needle lithographs'.

Lavín embroidery – which involves embroidering with hair – is considered a type of erudite embroidery because of its level of complexity. 'Lavín' is a variant of the Zaragozan name 'Lausín'; in Spain the work is better known as Lausín embroidery, but upon arriving in America it was changed to Lavín embroidery. Either of the two terms is correct.

In Mexico there was a tradition of Lavín embroidery in the 18th century. In Las Vizcaínas, the College of San Ignacio de Loyola, a Basque institution, this type of work was taught and worked onto courtship handkerchiefs, whereby a young woman used her fiancé's hair to accept a formal marriage proposal.

In China, embroidery with hair goes back to the Tang Dynasty (618–907), when the women embroidered images of Buddha as an offering of piety. This type of work was called *moxiu* embroidery, which means 'black'.

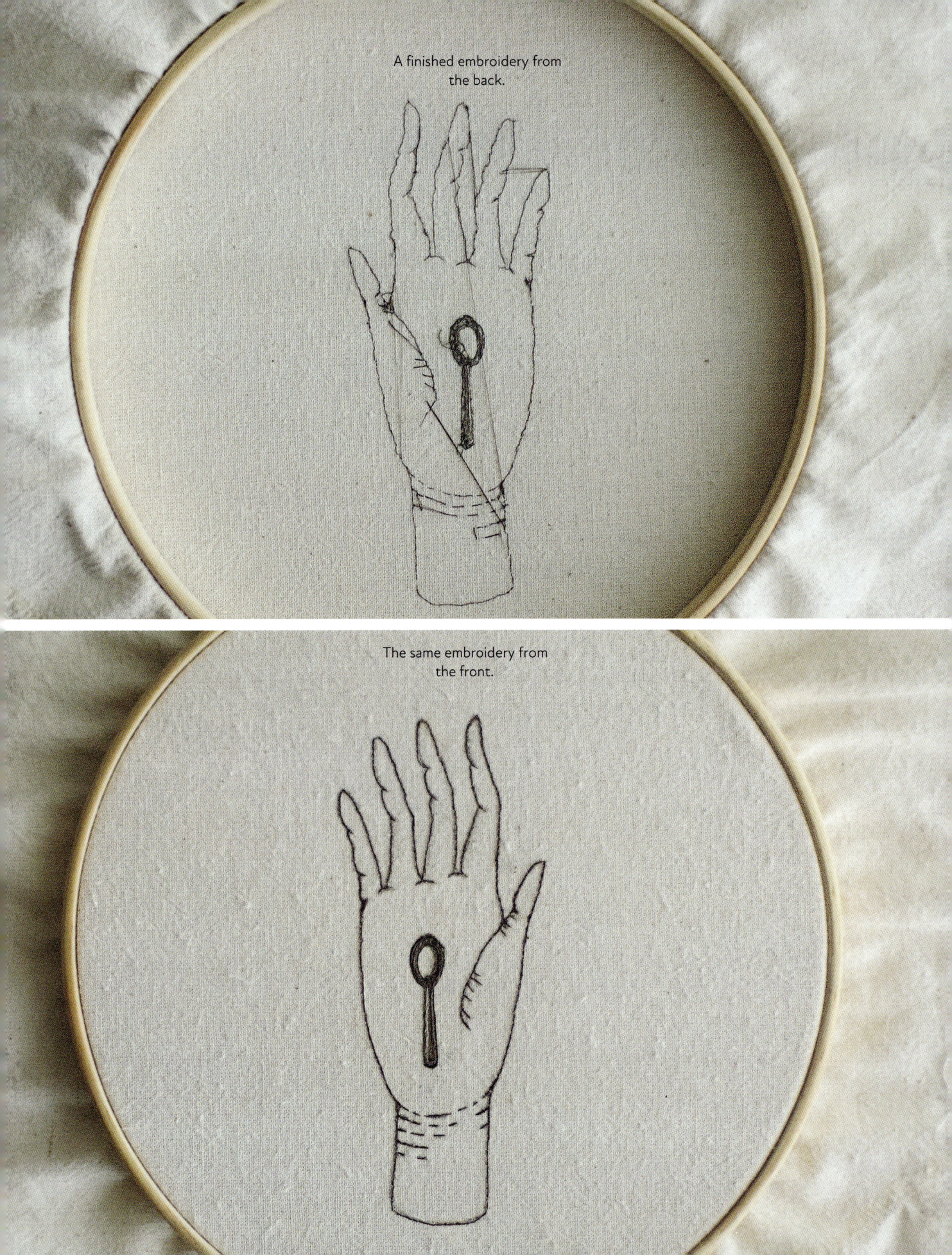

Lavín embroidery is normally presented in monochrome pieces, unless made with grey hair or other hair tones.

As soon as hair is removed from the scalp it begins to lose keratin. This makes it less elastic; over time the capillary walls become week, and the hair loses its structure, becoming thin and brittle until it can no longer be used for embroidery. Healthy hair retains its plasticity and elasticity for a year or a year and a half.

A good way of storing hair to be used for sewing is to braid it. Although this may curl it a bit, in this way it keeps better than in any other way.

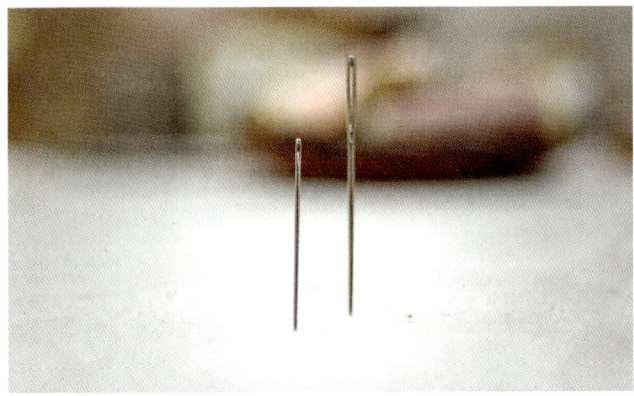
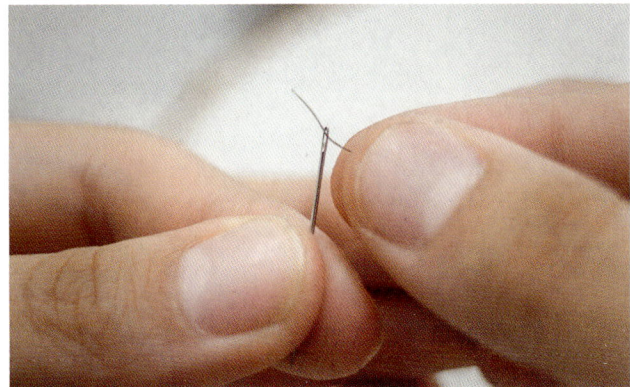
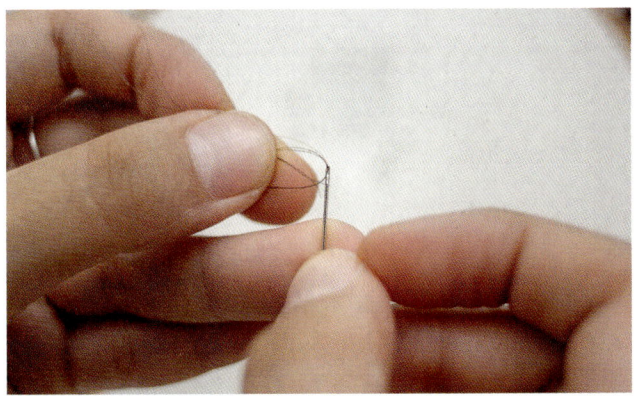
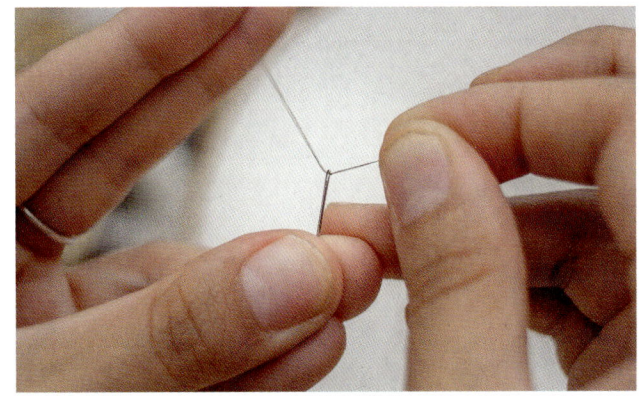
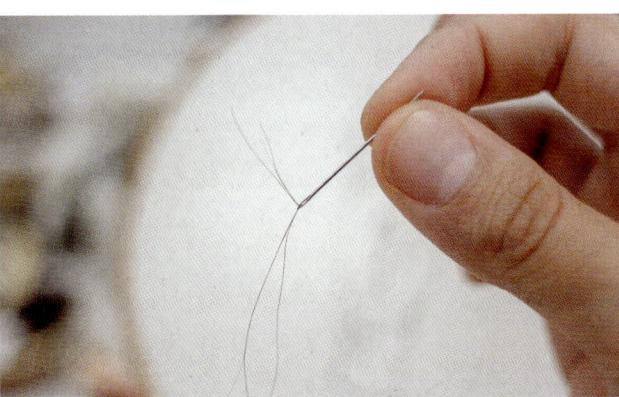

1. Choose a lock by feel and colour and secure it with a small elastic band, leaving a margin of approximately 4cm (1½in) in relation to the head for a good cut.

2. Make a classic plait of three strands, which is loose so as not to indent the hair too much. Secure at the end with another elastic band. **Note:** do not plait wet hair: when hair is wet, it is 50% more elastic and malleable so will curl a lot.

3. Cut carefully, leaving that 4cm (1½in) margin that we left at the start. Do this in front of a mirror.

To start, brush all of the hair well. Brushing will make it easier to handle, from starting to braid to embroidering.

First we have to establish what type of hair we have in order to know approximately what quantity we can cut and where. Hair does not grow uniformly over the whole head, and we need to identify where its growth is most abundant.

I prefer to cut locks from the base of the crown, as it is easily hidden with other hair, although this varies from person to person. Make sure that you cut strategically if you don't want the loss to show afterwards.

Some people treat their hair chemically after cutting it in order to use it for embroidery – it is conditioned, tinted and set. I prefer to use it as it comes. I have no problem if the hair has been treated by the person themself, but I don't treat the hair once it has been given to me. I prefer to keep the hair natural as a symbolic act. Because of this I call it 'live embroidery'.

In Lavín embroidery, what is important, apart from the stitch, is the technique. It is a type of work that requires impeccable application, otherwise it looks badly done. There is no middle ground.

In order to embroider with hair it is recommended that you use a needle with a short eye. To embroider, I personally prefer needles with a long eye, but a short eye – such as a dressmaking needle – helps me to secure the hair.

I always work from the root to the tip and do not tie a final knot. So to fix the hair to the needle and be able to work with it, I tie a knot at the eye of the needle (see the photos on page 155). The hair is so fine that this knot does not stop the needle from passing through the fabric.

To start I pick up a couple of threads from the fabric and go through the same location to secure the stitch.

From here I start to outline with backstitch (see pages 28–29). I always outline the whole of the shape first and then I decide where and how to infill.

The stitch that I use for this type of filling is the same one used in Toninero embroidery (see pages 112–119). You will have to be careful with thicknesses and types of hair as this varies even on the same person and will affect the resultant colour.

In Lavín embroidery the theory of colour is extremely interesting. One of the ways of introducing some variety, even in monochrome pieces, is through saturation of colour and for this grey hairs are ideal. A grey hair is not really a white hair but in fact a hair with no colour, a transparent hair. There are different tones of grey hair because the pigmentary cells (the cells that produce melanin) reduce their activity or die. A totally white hair is in fact just a hair that refracts light. As a result the best tone for introducing variety to hair is its own grey.

You can blend the colour, mixing the natural hair with white hair, or by selecting different colours of hair. In either of the two cases you have to choose hair by hair, and thread each needle with a different combination of hairs for a subtle gradient or to generate contrast.

In Lavín embroidery the chromatic graduation is limited but very rich. When the hair is not treated, the colour is perennial. I think of Lavín embroidery as a way of changing the perception of the world as we see it, by understanding more. Each line that I draw changes the texture of the fabric and, at the same time, redraws the image in my mind. It is a living image, changeable in its creation and inhabited in its body and its design. The embroidered image redraws the subject and changes my perception. I translate it, restructure it and inhabit it. With each stitch I extract a different being.

It is clear that the act of drawing mixes the perception, the memory and the sense that each person has of themself in life. An embroidery represents more than its actual subject. Embroidery is both a textile and physical drawing. Every drawing represents a testimony of time, body and life. Embroidery records how the world is lived, and the material becomes the medium through which it is lived.

A finished embroidery from the back.

The same embroidery from the front.

Compositions from texture

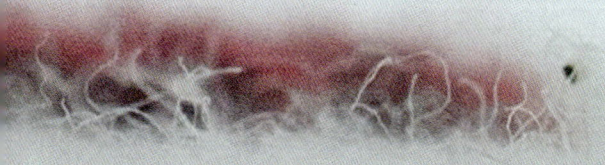

There are two types of artisan work: that of certainty and that of risk. In the first, the quality of the final product is structured from the start of the creation process and the hand cannot affect its mechanized structure. In the second, there is freedom in relation to accidents, inexperience and the probability that the creator will start to 'spoil' the work. Great works of art exist thanks to the work of risk, and it is on this principle that my work is based. Compositions formed around texture are based on this probability, as the gestural texture is the result of the work of risk in sewing.

Of course the certainty exists in hand embroidery too. We have diagrams, we can count each stitch, and the best-known, perfect pieces are the fruit of this type of work. There are undeniably stunning pieces, of impeccable workmanship.

Risk implies uncertainty, lack of control and, with it, the fear inherent in any exploration. But even here, in this book, risk is present – even in the logical and satisfying Mazahua embroidery. I think that it is also in the very concept of the piece, in the mind and in our bodies. Ultimately, hand embroidery can be like an extension of one's own body.

At the beginning of the book I talked about embroidery as an image. It is a work of lines, like engraving or drawing, as embroidery is graphic. But there is one element that makes embroidery a particularly sensorial technique. We perceive texture through touch; it is an invitation to caress. Even in the photographic record of embroidery, texture is fundamental, and this tactile richness is one of the most difficult elements to reproduce in a photograph.

I think of hand embroidery as a tactile immersion in which the hand touches, investigates and explores in an almost independent manner. In my work processes, artistic production is a form of mental, evocative and conceptual investigation. Through embroidery a non-verbal experience and knowledge is developed.

Composition based solely on texture is a deeply enriching process, engaging the sensations of touch, rhythm, colour and form, driven by a desire for continuity rather than any need for representation. In this way a dialogue is struck up, teaching us new ways of listening, to know when to stop or to know where to go.

Embroidery is more than simply stitches on fabric. In textile creation, the risk breathes in the atmosphere, and one forgets that one is embroidering. It is to submerge oneself in an abstract base, a general substance, an open knot. In embroidery, the mind needs to relax momentarily to give way to a mode of bodily exploration.

All materials contain tactile information. Fabric and paper are not so different (and both can be embroidered), although the feel of rice paper and cotton paper differ, as do paper and fabric, in that fabric has more elasticity.

It is important that the colour palette is very well chosen in these compositions so as not to compete with the texture, which is a more subtle element. It is like avoiding very strong flavours before trying something very delicate. In fact, colour is the most dominant element of an image. In risk embroidery the stitch appears in the fabric at the same time as a mental map is drawn of the piece, with the hand as the mediator. It is impossible to know which appears first, the stitch or the intention. The hands speak and listen at the same time in touch, in the caress, in the stitch, in the silence.

STITCHES
Moss

Moss stitch (similar to what we call seed stitch) is a type of infill with individual high-relief stitches. To achieve this high relief I usually use tapestry threads, but you can also make it easier for yourself by using a needle or a pin to give shape to the stitch before securing. Alternatively, use several strands of a mouliné thread.

When you embroider, think about each stitch individually, as if you were placing each one on the fabric.

1. Make small straight stitches on the fabric.

2. Use a needle or a pin to lift the stitch and give it shape and a bit of volume.

3. Secure the thread with a tiny, flat stitch or two. Remove the needle you used to shape the stitches with care.

4. Continue in this way for as long as you wish.

Play around with your colour palette. If you have it well defined from the start, you will not have to follow any order for it to look good.

A finished embroidery from the back.

The same embroidery from the front.

Cortés braid

The cortés braid (which you may know of by the names of braid stitch or cable plait stitch) is worked from top to bottom over guidelines of two parallel lines that will mark the edges of the braid.

Secure the thread on the back with a small knot.

Here, the cortés braid has been worked with two strands of a mouliné thread, but you can use more, or fewer, fepending on the finish you wish to achieve.

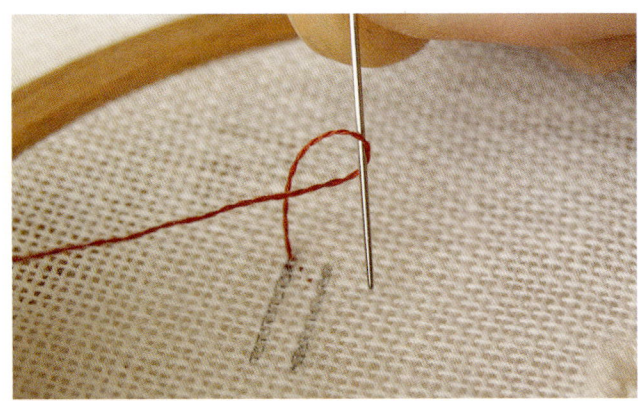

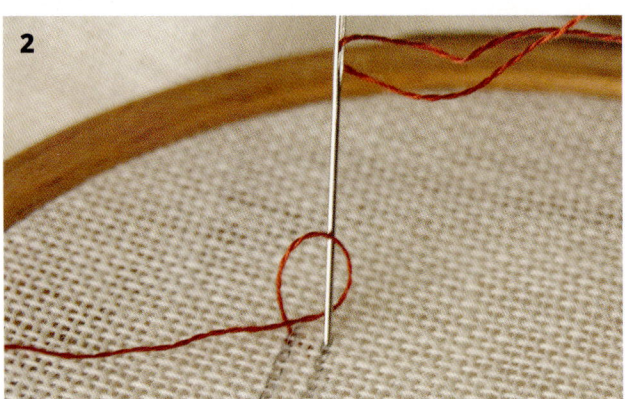

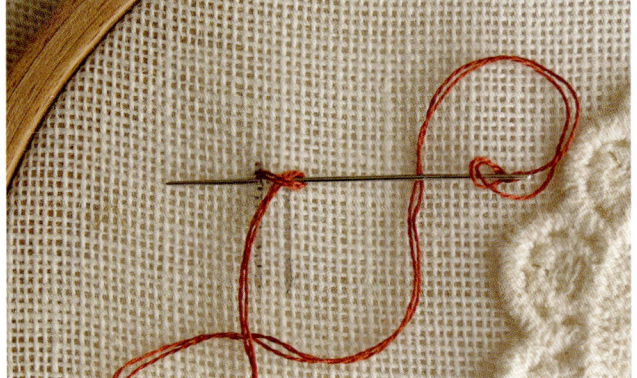

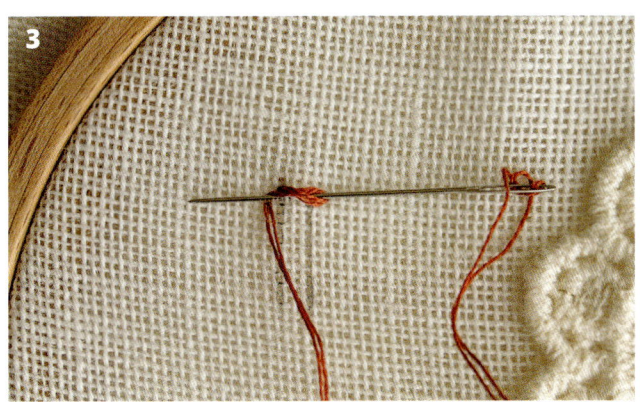

1. Bring the needle out on the left-hand line. With the working thread make a loop by twisting the needle downwards, as shown in the photograph.

2. Go across the fabric, insert the needle on the right-hand line and bring it out on the left-hand line, just below where the thread emerges.

3. Pass the working thread under the needle and pull through. This is the first stitch.

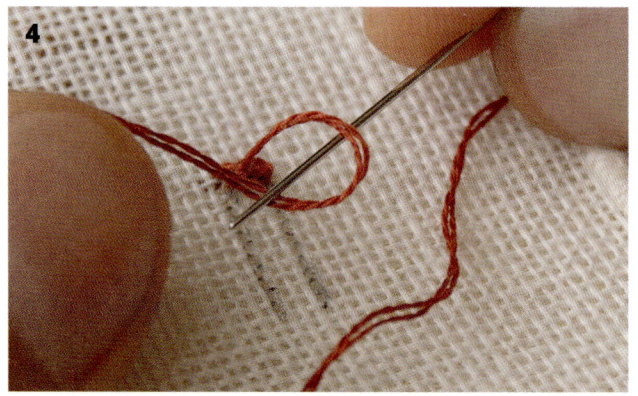

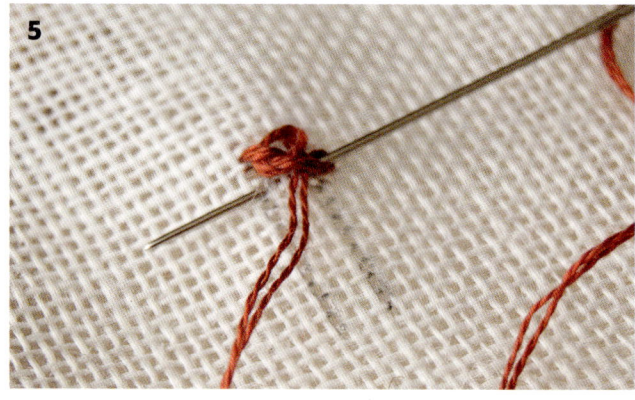

4. Take up the working thread again with the needle and make a loop by twisting the needle downwards (repeating step 1).

5. Take a stitch across the fabric from right to left, as before.

6. Pass the working thread under the needle and then pull through.

7. Continue in this way to achieve the size of the shape that you want.

8. Finish on the back by threading the needle under a few stitches and then trimming off the thread tail.

8

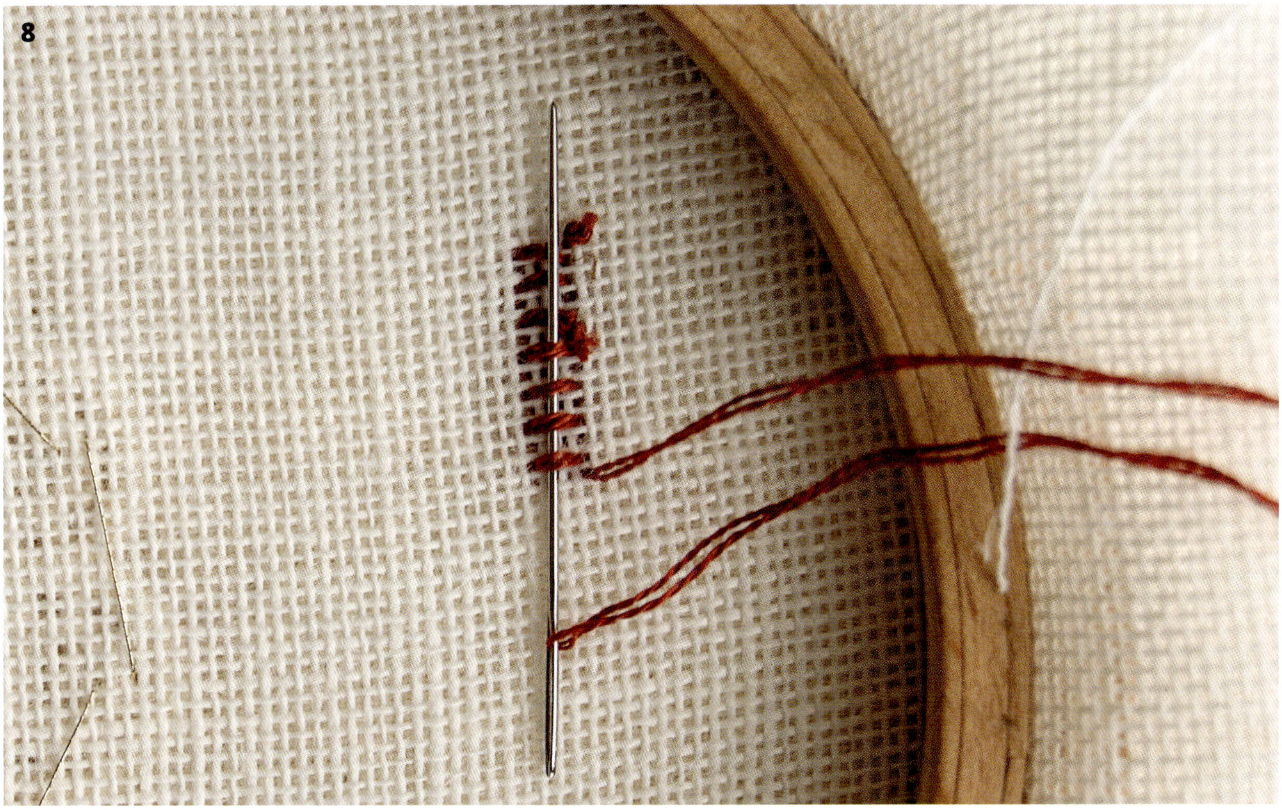

171

A finished embroidery from the back.

The same embroidery from the front.

French knot

Depending on your fabric you can use a sharp needle or a blunt needle – I like to use a sharp needle.

The size of the stitch will often depend more on the thickness of thread that you are using than the number of wraps you make.

Here, the French knot has been worked in a single strand of size 8 perlé thread on a size 22 needle.

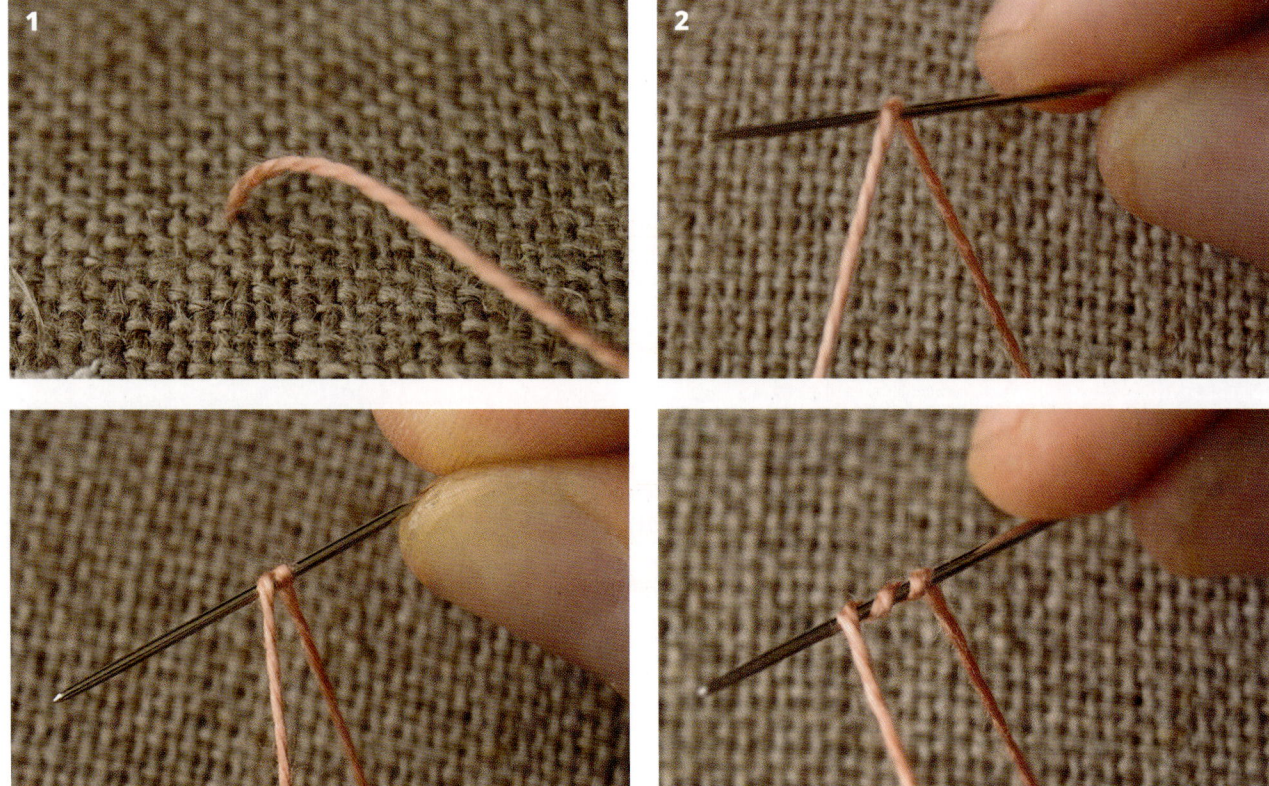

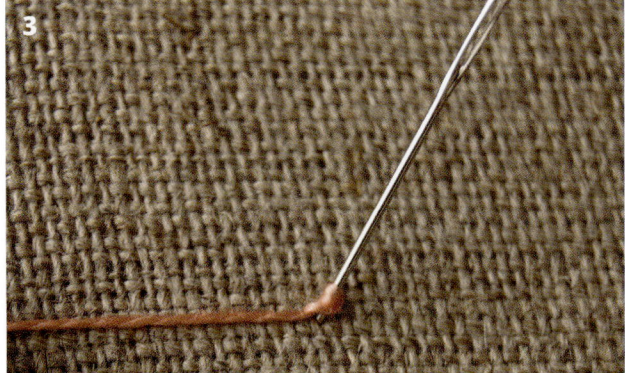

1. Bring the needle out where you want the knot to be.

2. Pass the working thread around the needle, once, twice, three times.

3. Take the needle back into the fabric where it came out, or close to it, making sure that the wraps are taut around the needle.

4. So that the French knot turns out nice and uniform, you have to keep the working thread tight. **Note:** keep the thread tight but not tense. The needle must slide through smoothly and without any problem.

4

Coral stitch

Mexican coral stitch is also known as feather stitch and can be worked intuitively, as here, or used for borders or fillings.

A size 22 tapestry needle has been used here, with a single strand of size 8 perlé thread.

1. Bring the needle out, take it back in to one side, at the same level as before, and bring it back out centred and further down, forming a triangle. Make sure that the working thread is under the needle.

2. From here repeat the previous step.

3. You will be forming 'little trees'.

4. You can plan your stitches to interweave colours.

177

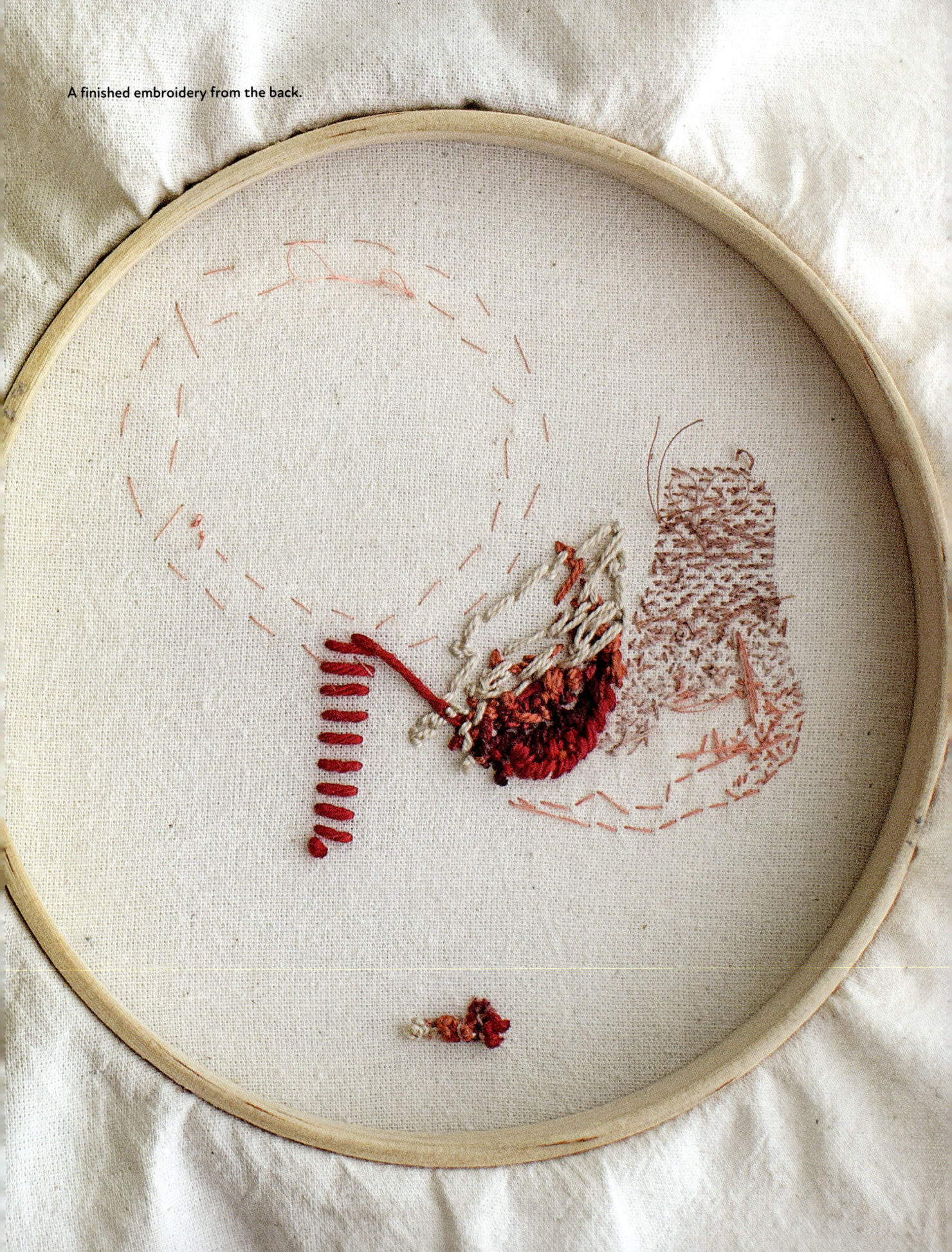
A finished embroidery from the back.

The same embroidery from the front.

Morse stitch

I started to use this stitch while looking for something that was extremely subtle, minimal. I discovered it by doing photo-embroidery (as shown opposite): I was looking for a stitch to complement the image with which it would be integrated.

I named this stitch as such because it reminds me of Morse code. Normally I do it with silk sewing thread or with hair, but in order to make the explanation easier I will use perlé – here, a single thread of size 8 on a blunt no. 22 needle.

The stitch is particularly effective on open-weave fabrics but can be worked on any fabric.

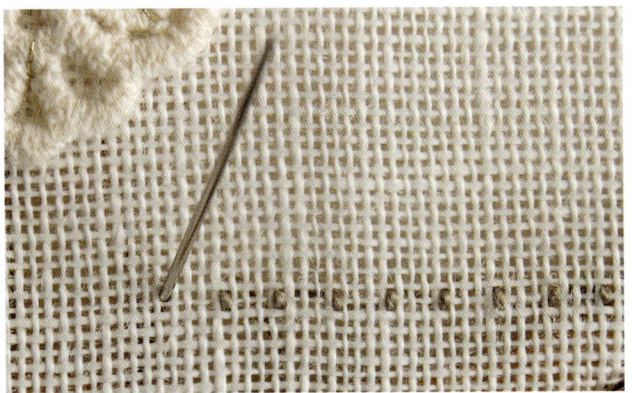

Bring the needle out of the fabric and make a small stitch, taking only a couple of threads, or three – as many as you think look good. Leave a space and take another stitch.

It is very simple; it is a matter of going in and out of the fabric. The important thing about this stitch and embroidery based on texture is the spacing. When I embroider I do not think about the thread and the stitch but the spaces that I am leaving and that's how I measure it. I get into a rhythm, one space, one space, two, one space, two, three, one, one. It is very intuitive – you almost let the thread decide.

TEMPLATES

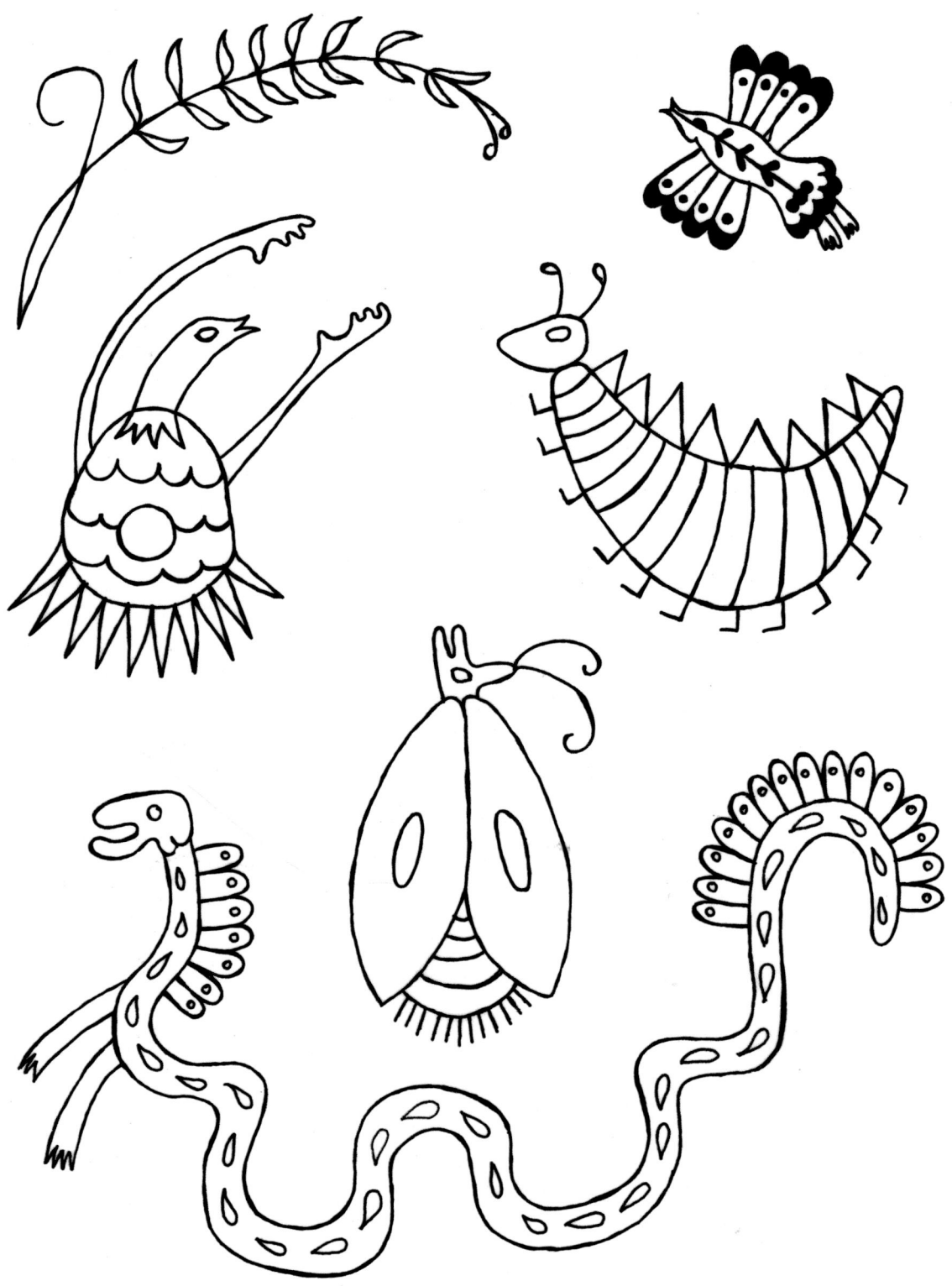

TENANGO EMBROIDERY
(see pages 20–41)

STREET EMBROIDERY
(see pages 42–71)

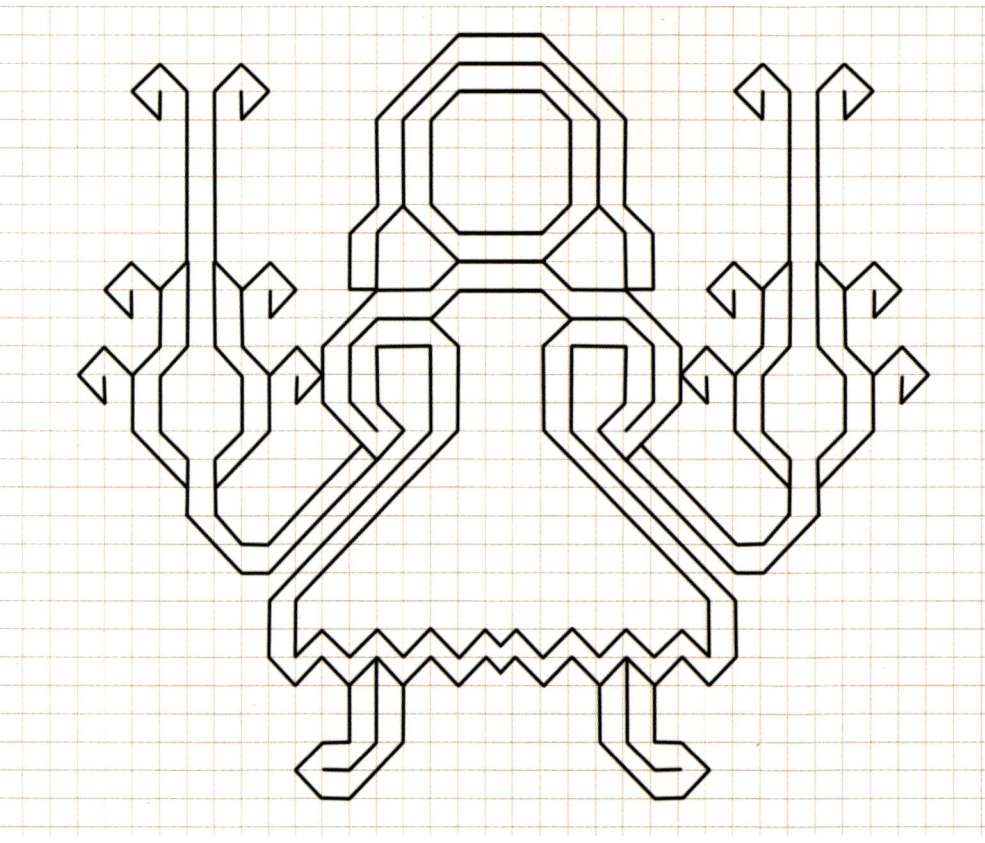
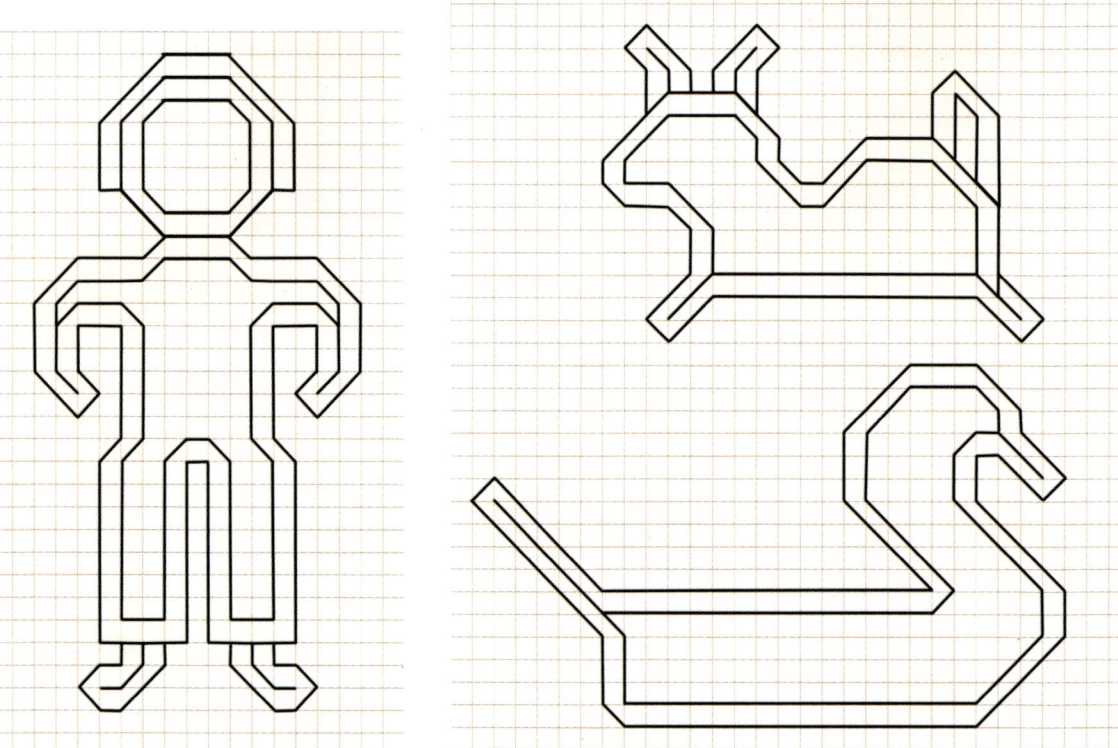

MAZAHUA EMBROIDERY
(see pages 72–111)

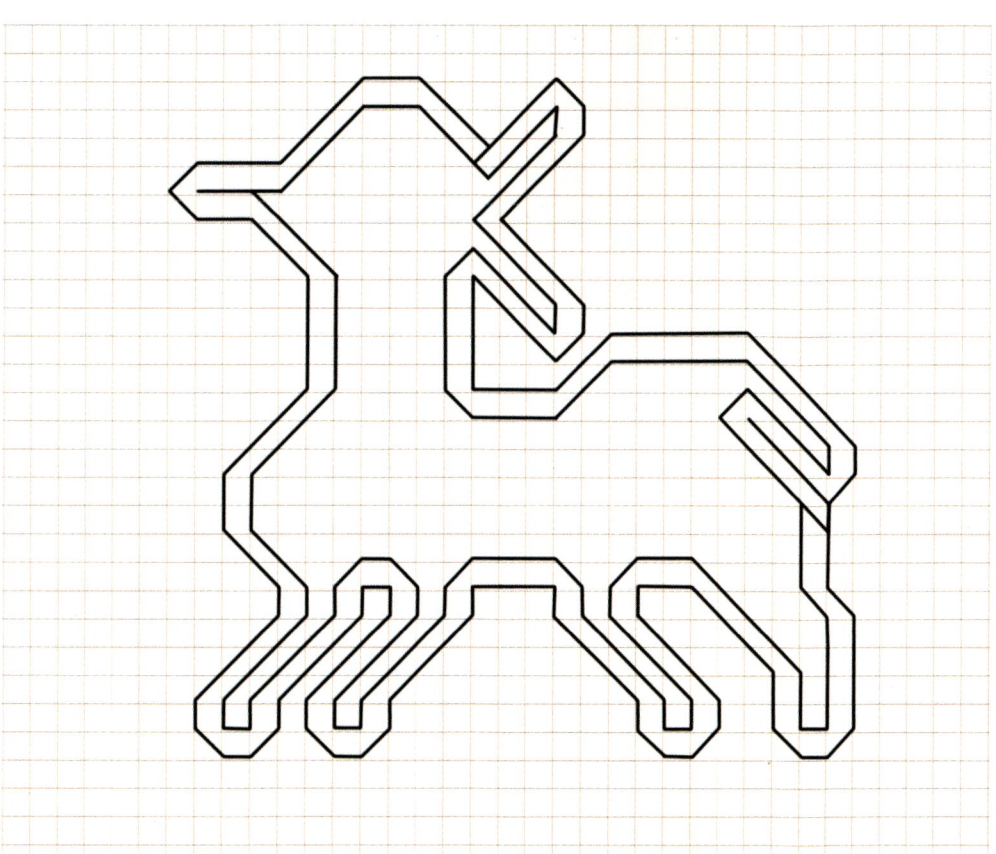

TONINERO EMBROIDERY
(see pages 112–121)

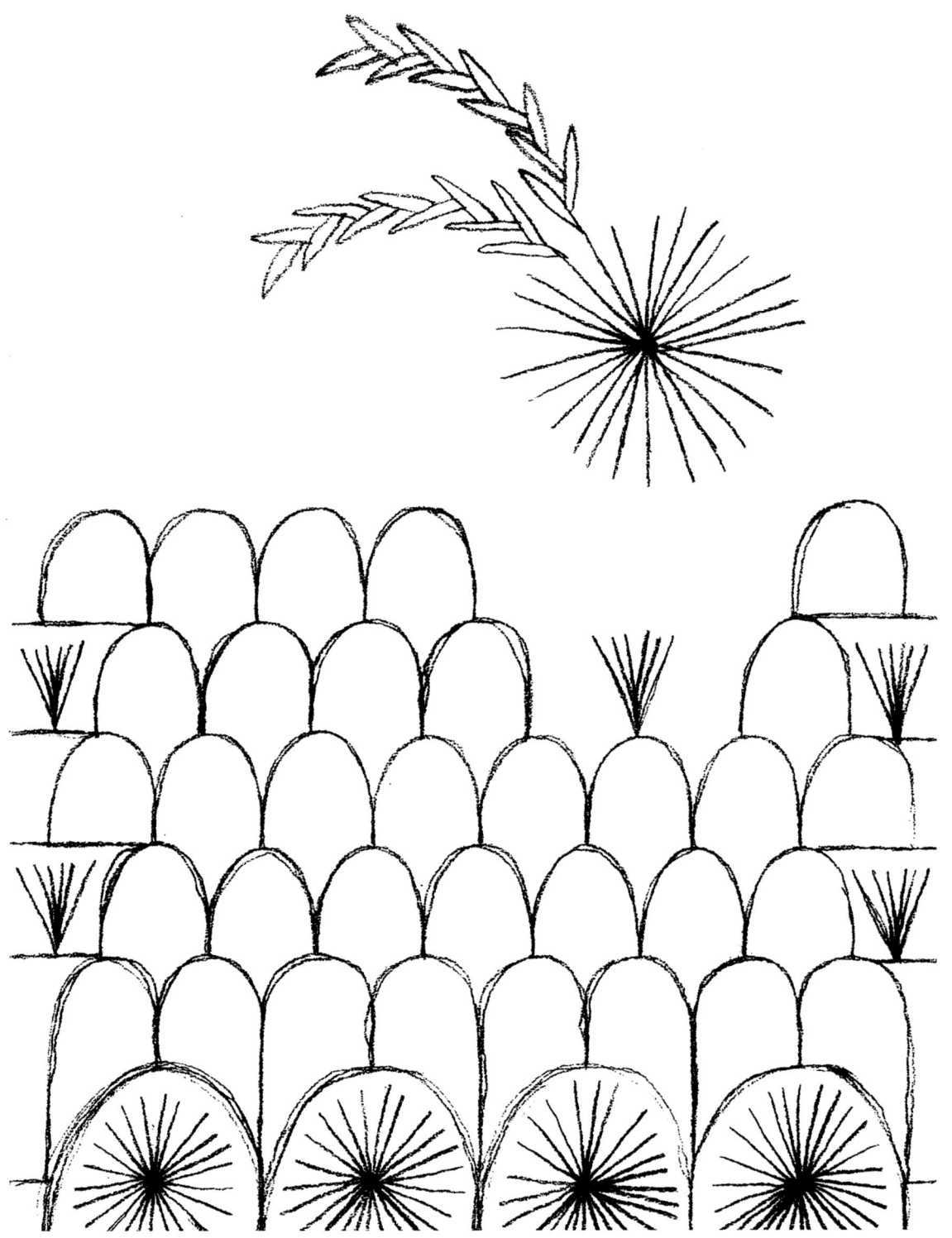

MIXE EMBROIDERY
(see pages 122–129)

PURÉPECHA EMBROIDERY
(see pages 130–149)

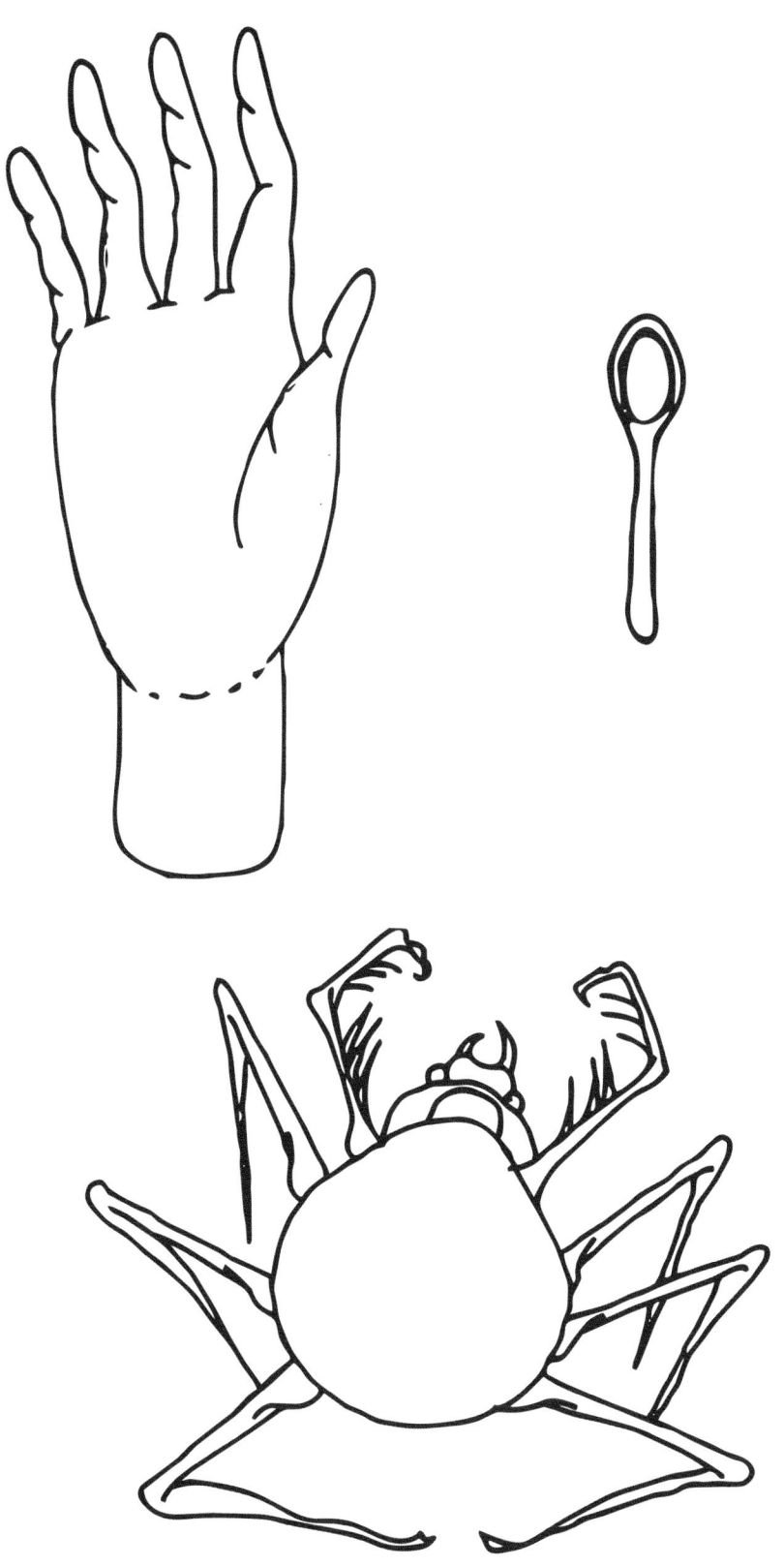

LAVÍN EMBROIDERY
(see pages 150–159)

Biography

Gimena Romero is an artist and illustrator who specializes in textile graphics. She was born in Mexico City in 1985 and currently lives between Mexico D.F. (now known as Mexico City) and Madrid. A graduate of plastic and visual arts from the Escuela Nacional de Pintura, Escultura y Grabado 'La Esmerelda', of the Instituto Nacional de Bellas Artes (INBA), she did part of her degree in arts at the École Nationale des Beaux Arts in Lyon, France. She has won numerous prizes and international mentions such as *Iberoamérica Ilustra* and *FILIJ Catálogo de Ilustración Mexicana*. In 2010 she was the cultural representative for Mexico in France with the Vargas Lugo prize and completed her textile training at the École Lesage.

In 2014 she did an internship to learn embroidery with gold threads in Seville (Spain), attaining the highest level in the technique. In 2013 she won first place in illustration for the 'Petirroja' series at the COW International Design Festival in Dnipropetrovsk, Ukraine. It was selected as one of the best embroidery projects in the world by Maison Bijoux. In 2015 she was awarded the Creación Jóven scholarship by INJUVE – Spain to create the series of *Canciones para terminar de otro modo* ('*Songs to finish in another way*'), in the context of Illustratour 2015. Her work has been included in various exhibitions around the world, including Mexico, Brazil, Argentina, France, Portugal, Ukraine and Spain.
She loves life, dogs and biscuits.

Web: estudiogimenaromero.com
Instagram: @gimenaromero
Facebook: Estudio Gimena Romero

Thanks

I want to thank with all my heart Pedro Aragón for lending me his eyes and enduring each one of the adventures involved in the creation of this book; Geraldine Padilla and Julieta Maldonado, who finally learned to embroider; Mónica Beck, for her talent, her affection and her appropriate words; all of the much-loved Beck clan, for being a positive family and giving me tons of affection; Mónica Gili, for her embroiderer's mind; and, of course, my parents and my brother, for taking on the role of bastion and stockade.

Embroiderers who have participated in this book

Mónica Beck
Julieta Maldonado
Geraldine Padilla
Jan Christian Ferrer
Pedro Aragón
Ana María Rodríguez
Gimena Romero

List of names and provenance of the embroideries

	REGION	COMMUNITY	NAME OF THE COMMUNITY IN ITS ORIGINAL LANGUAGE, AND MEANING	OTHER NAMES BY WHICH THIS TYPE OF EMBROIDERY IS ALSO KNOWN
TENANGO EMBROIDERY	Tenango de Doria, Hidalgo	Otomí	*Hñähñu* (Otomí language)	
STREET EMBROIDERY	Mexico City	Embroidery developed by the author		
MAZAHUA EMBROIDERY	San Felipe, Villa de Allende, Mexico state	Mazahua	*Mazahua* (Deer People)	
TONINERO EMBROIDERY	San Antonino Castillo Velasco, Oaxaca	Zapoteca	*Binnizá* ('People of the Clouds, the external space')	Toninero embroidery, San Antonino embroidery
MIXE EMBROIDERY	Santa María Tlahuitoltepec, Oaxaca	Mixe	*Ayüük* (Mixe language)	Tiahui embroidery
PURÉPECHA EMBROIDERY	Tzintzuntzan, Pátzcuaro-Zirahuén, Michoacán	Purépecha	*P'urhépecha* The word *p'urhépecha* means 'war assistant', which is strange, as it as an imperial town. From this it is believed that the correct term would be '*achéecha*', although the official term is *Purépecha*.	Hummingbird embroidery
LAVÍN EMBROIDERY	Mexico City	Embroidery developed by the author		Lausín embroidery, embroidery with hair
COMPOSITIONS FROM TEXTURE	Mexico City	Embroidery developed by the author		Compositions based around texture are part of the textile investigation that the author has undertaken as an evocative language for nine years.

First published in the UK in 2026
by Search Press Limited
Wellwood, North Farm Road,
Tunbridge Wells, Kent TN2 3DR

1 2 3 4 5 6 7 8 9 10

Original title: *México bordado*, published by Editorial GG, Barcelona, Spain, 2017.

© Gimena Romero, 2017
Photography © Pedro Aragón, 2017
This edition is published by arrangement with Editorial GG.

English translation from the original Spanish by Burravoe Translation Services.

All rights reserved. No part of this book, text or images may be reproduced or transmitted in any physical or electronic form known or as yet unknown, or used or reproduced in any manner for the purpose of training artificial intelligence technologies or systems, without written permission obtained beforehand from Search Press. Readers are permitted to reproduce any of the projects in this book for their personal use, or for the purpose of selling for charity, free of charge and without the prior permission of the Publishers. You are not permitted to use any of the projects or artworks for commercial purposes.

ISBN: 978-1-80092-418-5
ebook ISBN: 978-1-80093-376-7

Bookmarked Hub
For further ideas and inspiration, and to join our free online community, visit www.bookmarkedhub.com

Publishers' notes
Metric measurements are used in this book; the imperial conversions are rounded to the nearest ¼in. Always use either metric or imperial measurements, not a combination of both.

The Publishers and author can accept no responsibility for any consequences arising from the information, advice or instructions given in this publication.

For errata, please visit our website (www.searchpress.com) or the Bookmarked Hub (www.bookmarkedhub.com).

GPSR information can be found at www.searchpress.com
Printed in China, TT022026

You are invited to visit the author's website: www.estudiogimenaromero.com
Instagram: @gimenaromero
Facebook: Estudio Gimena Romero